e Re

CARLYLE'S FUSION OF
POETRY, HISTORY, AND RELIGION

CARLYLE'S FUSION OF POETRY, HISTORY, AND RELIGION BY 1834

By HILL SHINE

KENNIKAT PRESS, INC./PORT WASHINGTON, N. Y.

Copyright 1938 by The University of North Carolina Press
Reissued in 1967 by Kennikat Press by arrangement

Library of Congress Catalog Card No: 67-27649

Manufactured in the United States of America

FOREWORD

A student of the transition of thought in the nineteenth century is fortunate when he turns to the developing Carlyle. For the records are unusually full. And for the most part they are accessible. Like many of his contemporaries, Carlyle attempted to assimilate some of the new gains in systematic philosophy, in social theory, and in the conceptions of poetry, history, and religion. Although the outcomes of his attempts differ—sometimes in degree, sometimes in kind—from the general transitions of thought that occurred in his century, the attempts themselves are significant of his time. And for an understanding of Carlyle as an individual, they are basic.

A case in point is the development that Carlyle's conceptions of religion, poetry, and history underwent. By 1834, he had attempted to fuse the three conceptions. An important clue to that phase of his development is the principle of tolerance. His definition of the principle occurred early. It was prepared for by an adaptation of *reason* from German philosophy, and was appropriated from the progressive tradition current in Germany, France, and Britain. And he attempted to apply it in spite of his Calvinistic inheritance. The implications and conflicts of that principle of tolerance run through many years of his life and many volumes of his works. Both the development and the early application of that principle, among others, will be discussed in detail in the pages that follow.

This study of Carlyle's fusion of religion, poetry, and history was conceived and executed as a whole three years ago. But because of the difficulties of publication, it was made into three articles. And the three were published serially during the years 1936 and 1937 in *Studies in Philology*.[1] Now that publication as a whole has become possible, I am allowing the material to stand almost entirely as it was first printed. The first article, " Carlyle's Views on the Relation between Religion and Poetry up to 1832," discusses Carlyle's definitions of reason and tolerance, and shows how they led up to his theoretical fusion of religion and poetry. The second article, " Carlyle's Views on the Relation between Poetry and History up to early 1832," presents the development of his interest in

[1] XXXIII (1936), 57-92; 487-506; XXXIV (1937), 438-466.

history and society, the waning of his interest in systematic philosophy, and his definition of realism so as to identify poetry and history. The last article, "Carlyle's Fusion of Poetry, History, and Religion by 1834," takes up the converging theories of religion, poetry, and history which he had developed by 1832 and traces them through the vicissitudes of the next two years until he practically exemplified the fusion of the three in his composition *The Diamond Necklace*. As will be seen, all three of the original articles prepared for, and bear upon, the central problem of that three-fold fusion. Therefore the present method of publication—reprinting the articles together and inserting additional page-references within the footnotes—should not cause any confusion to a reader.

I wish to express my gratitude to the Editor of *Studies in Philology*, Professor George R. Coffman, for helpful criticism and for permission to re-print; to my colleagues at Maryville College, Professors E. R. Hunter and H. E. Orr, for reading the manuscript and making valuable suggestions, and Miss Clemmie J. Henry and her assistants for patient copying; to President R. W. Lloyd and Maryville College for encouragement and financial aid; to Miss Georgia H. Faison, Reference Librarian at the University of North Carolina, for skillful and untiring cooperation during many years; to Helen Chadwick Shine for help of all kinds; and especially to Professor John Manning Booker, to whose insight, inspiration, and guidance, this study is largely due and to whom it is therefore fittingly dedicated.

CONTENTS

CARLYLE'S VIEWS ON THE RELATION BETWEEN
RELIGION AND POETRY UP TO 1832

This article attempts to trace the development of Carlyle's views on the relation between religion and poetry up to the end of his 36th year. As will be shown, two decisive factors in these views were his conception of reason and his principle of tolerance. These factors will be discussed in the order stated. First, his change from condemnation of reason to approval of it will be traced up to the point at which, in a published essay, he considered reason the foundation of religion and poetry. Second, the development of the principle of tolerance will be discussed up to the point at which he published a clear statement of his use of this principle in his literary criticism. And, then, his thought upon the comparative value of religion and poetry will be presented up to the point at which he realized that his conflict was between two moral systems and that the principle of tolerance was a decisive factor in this conflict.

No detailed exposition will be here attempted of Carlyle's indebtedness to German philosophy, of his critical theory in literature, or of his religious tenets. Studies of these separate elements in his intellectual development are already available.[1] This par-

---

[1] Since Isaac Watson Dyer's *A Bibliography of Thomas Carlyle's Writings and Ana* (Portland, Maine, 1928) and the annual "Victorian Bibliography" (compiled by W. D. Templeman and others in the Victorian Group of M. L. A. and published in the May numbers of *MP*) are accessible, only a few of the titles need be listed here.

German Philosophy: Margaret Storrs, *The Relation of Carlyle to Kant and Fichte* (Bryn Mawr, Pa., 1929). See especially pp. 27-29, 41-43, 52, 61-62, 68-69, 73, 80-81, 88, 97-100. B. H. Lehman, *Carlyle's Theory of the Hero* (Durham, N. C., 1928). See especially pp. 103-123. René Wellek, *Immanuel Kant in England: 1793-1838* (Princeton, N. J., 1931). See especially pp. 182, 188-189, 200-201. C. F. Harrold, "Carlyle's Interpretation of Kant," *PQ*, VII (1928), 345-357. See especially 345-349, 350, 353, 357. The conclusions of this and of several other articles by Professor Harrold are presented and further developed in his recent book on Carlyle and German thought: C. F. Harrold, *Carlyle and German Thought: 1819-1834* (Yale Studies in English, LXXXII, New Haven, 1934). See especially Chapter V: "Understanding, Reason, Phantasy," pp. 120-150. The present

ticular study touches these elements, it is true, but only incidentally. Its special function is to trace the growth of Carlyle's views concerning the relations of religion and poetry, rather than to present his philosophic, literary, or religious creed.

I. Reason

One of the important results of Carlyle's study of German philosophy was a conception that poetry and religion belonged to, and were united in, the province of reason, *Vernunft*. This association between art and religion survived his interest in the philosophy that provided it. Although he eventually renounced both his pseudo-German conception of reason, and philosophic speculation in general, the fact that a favorable conception of reason served as an early union between poetry and religion would alone make the development of the favorable attitude toward reason in Carlyle's mind an important part of this discussion.

Early in his intellectual development Carlyle entertained a profound distrust of the human faculty, reason. He seems to have adopted the well-worn notion that head and heart were opposed to each other. His use of the terms was in part the same use that remains popular today. That is, *head* connoted reason or intellect; *heart* connoted conscience, virtuous feeling, and the sense of proper conduct. Sometimes he even seems to have stretched the term *heart* to include orthodoxy of faith. It is not certain when he first used this distinction between *head* and *heart*. But the sequence of events that prepared him for a hostile view of reason is clear. And it is long. Soon after he went to Edinburgh University in 1809

writer's article " Carlyle and the German Philosophy Problem during the Year 1826-1827," *PMLA*, L (1935), 807-827.

Literary Criticism: F. W. Roe, *Carlyle as a Critic of Literature* (N. Y., 1910). See especially pp. 71, 102, 137, 139-143 (Chapter IX: " From Criticism to Prophecy "), 144, 147.

Religion: J. A. Froude, *Thomas Carlyle. A History of the First Forty Years . . . 1795-1835* (N. Y., 1882). See especially II, 2. J. A. Froude, *Thomas Carlyle. A History of His Life in London: 1834-1881* (N. Y., 1884). See especially I, 11-12, 77. Ewald Flügel, *Thomas Carlyle's religiöse und sittliche Entwicklung und Weltanschauung* (Leipzig, 1887). See especially pp. 131-144, 149, 155-157, 166. Because of lack of knowledge of the Swedish language, I have been unable to read Knut Hagberg's *Thomas Carlyle. Romantik och Puritanism i Sartor Resartus* (Stockholm, 1925).

he must have become aware that in the intellectual world there were currents of thought which did not harmonize with the faith of his parents. Apparently in the summer of 1811, while he was home from his second year at the University, he asked his mother the reasonable question, whether God Almighty actually came down to earth and made wheelbarrows in a shop. This question, and others like it, were answered only by the unconvincing logic of tears.[2] Thus he learned to keep his questions to himself.

Intellectually unsatisfied though he was, he continued his preparation for the Presbyterian ministry. Three years later, December, 1814, he preached his first trial sermon.[3] It was so successful that early in 1815 he began preparations for his second sermon. This time the topic was the dangerous one *Num detur religio naturalis?*[4] The sermon gave satisfaction to the authorities, but the young man's intellect had not been convinced. He did not find sufficient evidence in physical nature to prove to him the existence of a spiritual Providence.[5] Still later, at Kirkcaldy, he read the French writers of the Enlightenment.[6] And Hume and Gibbon had their share too in turning him from orthodoxy.[7] Finally, by early 1818, the faith in which he was born had been completely broken down.[8] Rationalism had done one part of its work in undermining dogmatic theology. But thus far, in Carlyle's case, it had failed to

---

[2] William Allingham, *A Diary*. Edited by H. Allingham and D. Radford (London, 1907), pp. 253 and 267-268. D. A. Wilson, *Carlyle till Marriage* (London, 1923), pp. 78-79, gives the summer of 1810 as the date of the wheelbarrow incident.

[3] Christmas, 1814. Thomas Carlyle, *Reminiscences*. Edited by C. E. Norton (London, 1887), II, 20. David Masson, *Edinburgh Sketches and Memoirs* (London, 1892), pp. 253-254.

[4] D. A. Wilson, *op. cit.*, p. 109. Thomas Carlyle, *Reminiscences*, II, 20. David Masson, *op. cit.*, p. 254.

[5] William Allingham, *A Diary*, p. 232.

[6] Thomas Carlyle, *Reminiscences*, II, 28-29. Thomas Carlyle, *Lectures on the History of Literature*. Edited by J. Reay Greene (second edition, London, 1892), p. 205.

[7] Thomas Carlyle, *Early Letters of Thomas Carlyle*. Edited by C. E. Norton (London, 1886), I, 20, 127, 133, 143-145, 146. Thomas Carlyle, *Reminiscences*, II, 28. David Masson, *op. cit.*, pp. 263-264. William Allingham, *A Diary*, pp. 232.

[8] In addition to the references given in the preceding note, see *Early Letters of Thomas Carlyle*, I, 96-99, 108, 162.

replace this loss. In many European minds rationalism had built up a conception of religion, morality, civilization, art, as gradual developments of an advancing humanity. Thus the *fiat* conception of the act of creation had been replaced by the conception of an evolutionary development:—the static had given way to the progressive. But not so in Carlyle's case, yet. His old procedure of destructive questioning went on in his mind, he said, for ten years after the wheelbarrow incident. And his far-wandering thoughts brought him no peace.

Under these conditions, he was prepared to feel deep sympathy with Faust, who had lost his salvation through an ambitious intellect. It was in the summer of 1820 that, with great emotion, Carlyle first read Goethe's *Faust* in the German.[9] And, at the beginning of 1822, he wrote his first critical article on German literature. Goethe's *Faust* was the subject. In this review Carlyle was attempting to deal with his own impasse of heart *versus* head. The opening scenes of the play seemed to him a portrayal of the agitation incident to " the destruction of a noble spirit by the force of its own thoughts. . . ."[10] Turned back from each effort to divine the essence of things, Faust finds the universe

a dark entangled riddle, the meaning of which, if it have any, is impenetrably hid from men. Nor is it to *know* only that he strives; the sensibilities of his heart have been embarked in this undertaking as well as the faculties of his intellect—he would *feel* as well as understand. . . .[11]

[He was] born with the head of a sceptic and the heart of a devotee; in grasping at the sublime, he has lost even the useful; when his earthly hopes are all blasted, no moral consolation is in store for him. . . .[12]

---

[9] On June 3, 1820, he wrote Irving that Goethe's gayety of head and melancholy of heart had opened up the floodgates of his sympathy. See " Unpublished Letters of Carlyle," *Scribner's Magazine*, XIII (1893), 417. See what may be an allusion to the conflict between head and heart in the letter of August 14, 1821, to Irving about Schiller, *ibid.*, 419. But on September 1, 1821, in a letter to his pupil, Miss Welsh, he seems to praise reason, considering mental excellence the highest of human attainments. *The Love Letters of Thomas Carlyle and Jane Welsh.* Edited by Alexander Carlyle (New York, 1909), I, 12.

[10] Thomas Carlyle, *Essay on Goethe's Faust* (Reprinted from *The* [*New*] *Edinburgh Review* . . . 1822. With an introduction by Richard Schroeder [N. Y. Knickerbocker Press, n. d.]), p. 40.

[11] *Ibid.*, 16.   [12] *Ibid.*, 41.

Faust's crimes are many, but his will seems to have had little share in them; even after his connection with the fiend, he feels virtuously, even nobly, though he acts ill; and, when we see Mephistopheles at length succeed in ruining a being so greatly his superior in all respects, it seems as if the spirit of evil were made victorious over that of good, the lower part of man's nature over the higher. But if such be our feeling, it is not with the poet that we must quarrel. "The soul that sinneth, it shall die" is the law of nature as well as of revelation; and acts of desperate rashness, though without any purpose morally bad in the author of them, as they produce fatal consequences to the individual or to others, must be punished accordingly. Faust's criminality existed long before he forsook his retirement, or addicted himself to the converse of spirits; it began when he allowed his desires to reach beyond the boundaries wherewith nature had circumscribed them, when he allowed his mind to wander—even in the search of truth—till it doubted the existence of a Providence, and the foundation of moral distinctions. All his subsequent miseries and crimes originated in this—at first view, so pardonable a transgression. . . . [13]

Still another passage shows Carlyle's denunciation of intellect and his identification of intellect with contempt for moral distinctions, with Mephistopheles, with French *philosophes,* and with mockery. He believed that Mephistopheles's conduct proceeded chiefly from

an utter contempt of moral distinctions. . . . His aim with Faust seems rather that of an *amateur,* than of a regular demon: he tempts him chiefly as an intellectual recreation. . . . In many respects Mephistopheles resembles some French *philosophe* of the last century. There is the perfection of the intellectual faculties with a total absence of the moral. . . . He [Mephistopheles] cannot pity, or admire, or worship—he can only mock. His presence is like a moral Harmattan, the "mortifying wind" of the desert, under which every green thing is parched and dies.

From the moment when Faust connects himself with such a being, his character and conduct become degraded. . . . [14]

Truly, to Carlyle in January, 1822, man's intellect seemed to be at war with his spiritual peace.[15]

During the spring of 1822, while engaged in a study of Milton and other Civil War figures, Carlyle made some significant notebook entries concerning reason. The first of these notes that need to be examined in this connection was written on March 25th or 26th, after reading Milton's first *Pro Populo Anglicano Defensio.*

---

[13] *Ibid.,* 42-43.   [14] *Ibid.,* 25, 26, 27.

[15] On February 26, 1822, in a letter to Miss Welsh, he continued to associate intellect with the infernal powers. *The Love Letters of Thomas Carlyle and Jane Welsh,* I, 32-33.

Milton's mode of reasoning has something curious in it: he appeals to no first principles hardly. . . . Are *our* "first principles" more solid than his? I doubt if they are *so* much more, as we often think. Nine tenths of our reasonings are *artificial* processes, depending not on the real nature of things but on our peculiar mode of viewing things, and therefore varying with all the variations both in the kind and extent of our perceptions. How is this? Truth *immer* WIRD *nie* IST? [16]

Here Schiller's German phrase, *wird, nie ist* is used for Carlyle's first expression of the Phoenix idea, which in *Sartor Resartus* he applied not simply to truth but to all social institutions as well. And, as a still further anticipation of *Sartor Resartus,* even the figurative language concerning clothes emerges on May 6th in a note written after reading Milton's *Areopagitica.*

The perusal of these old giants, and the infirm appearance of their most venerable structures in the department of philosophy & controversy ought surely to make us humble in our estimate of human Reason. *How* is it? The art of Logic seems to come & go & change like the fashion of clothes from age to age! [17]

These half-guesses about the changing forms in which reasoning appeared, represented, in fact, a great gain in Carlyle's method of thinking. He was on the track of the idea that truth is never an absolute accomplishment but is an infinite progressive development. He was taking steps in the direction of the great idea of progress that had emerged in European thought during the preceding century.[18]

But he did not yet have confidence in reason as a revealer of the

---

[16] Thomas Carlyle, *Two Note Books*, edited by C. E. Norton (N. Y.: Grolier Club, 1898), p. 4. Toward the end of 1831, in the essay "Characteristics," Carlyle assigned the Germanism in the last sentence of this quotation to Schiller. Thomas Carlyle, *Critical and Miscellaneous Essays*, edited by H. D. Traill (London, 1899), III, 38.

[17] Carlyle, *Two Note Books*, p. 30.

[18] See J. B. Bury, *The Idea of Progress*, Introduction by Charles A. Beard (N. Y., 1932), especially pp. 66, 109-110, 127-28, 134-37, 144-45, for the implications of this idea of progress. For supplement and correction to Bury, see Ronald S. Crane, "Anglican Apologetics and the Idea of Progress, 1699-1745." *MP*, XXXI (1934), 273-306 and 349-382, especially pp. 281, 362, 366, 368-369, 371-373, 379-380, 381-382. For additional treatment of the ramifications and developments of this idea, see Lois Whitney, *Primitivism and the Idea of Progress* (Baltimore, 1934). For a discussion of Carlyle's connection with this idea, see C. F. Harrold, *Carlyle and German Thought*, pp. 108-116, 155-168, 171-176.

kind of truth that could be followed in the conduct of life. This uncertainty appeared in a notebook entry of April 13, 1822. He had just finished reading the autobiography of the Quaker, Thomas Ellwood, one-time reader of Latin to Milton. Among other things in the book, Carlyle found a new phase of human nature. He found that, in spite of untoward circumstances, Ellwood's

heart was clear & healthful, and his life may justly be called happy notwithstanding. What made it so? How came he to shew so complete and consistent & respectable a walk and conversation amid so many drawbacks & obstructions? His *creed* was his support, his all in all. Is it better then to have *a* straight road formed for us, tho' a false one, thro' this confused wilderness of things—than to be waiting asking searching for a true one, if we never find it altogether? Compare Ellwood, a weak man, with Alfieri, Goethe, Voltaire, strong men; & award the palm! What *is* the proper province of Reason? [19]

In this passage Carlyle put the question of the superiority of heart or head. Although reason was under fire, and had been under fire for months, it is clear that reason had excellent advocates,—Alfieri, Goethe, and Voltaire.[20]

Another biographical project, started during the next spring, 1823, provides further evidence of Carlyle's attitude toward reason. Fortunately for the execution of this project, *The Life of Schiller,* Carlyle had adequate time in which to cultivate his understanding and sympathy for the German poet. The biography was written piecemeal during almost a year, and was published as a serial in *The London Magazine.* Then, still another year elapsed before he finished his revision of the work for its publication as a book. During these two years of intermittent occupation with Schiller, Carlyle's attitude in general underwent change. A good example of this change occurs in the final section of the magazine version, which was completed early in February, 1824.[21] It recalls to the reader's mind the problem that Carlyle had left unsolved two years before. As has been seen, on April 13, 1822, he had wondered

[19] Carlyle, *Two Note Books,* pp. 21-22.

[20] Although it introduces no new element into the consideration, a letter written on June 2 may have some interest. In it, Carlyle supported duty as superior to " all the mere *learning* which School or College ever taught." *Early Letters of Thomas Carlyle,* II, 82.

[21] For evidence of completion between the dates January 25 and February 8, 1824, see *The Love Letters of Thomas Carlyle and Jane Welsh,* I, 332-334.

which was preferable—to side with the weak Ellwood and follow a straight though false road through the wilderness of things, or to side with strong Alfieri, Goethe, or Voltaire and seek forever the true road in spite of uncertain consequences. Now, by early 1824, the case of Schiller convinced him that the false road was to be avoided at any cost.

Truth with Schiller, or what seemed such, was an indispensable requisite: if he but suspected an opinion to be false, however dear it may have been, he seems to have examined it with rigid scrutiny, and if he found it guilty, to have plucked it out, and resolutely cast it forth. The sacrifice might cause him pain, permanent pain; real damage, he imagined, it could hardly cause him. It is irksome and dangerous to travel in the dark; but better so, than with an *Ignis-fatuus* to guide us.[22]

Although Carlyle did not restate the problem as precisely as before and call it a question of heart or head, nevertheless this passage constitutes a decision on the issue between heart and head. In this passage, he had decided in favor of head. That is, in 1824 he shifted his preference from heart to head. But he had not reached the solution yet.

Another of the great changes to be observed in Carlyle's mind while he was at work upon this biography is his change of attitude toward Schiller's aesthetic speculations. Three brief illustrations, separated from each other by one-year intervals, will suffice. In March, 1823, Carlyle considered aesthetic speculations nonsense.[23] During February of the next year, he grudgingly admitted that the doctrine set forth in Schiller's aesthetic essays could be comprehended, by the aid of long study.[24] And, at the beginning of 1825, he gave them enthusiastic approval and desired to translate them, along with Schiller's other works, into English.[25] Thus, within two years, Carlyle's attitude toward Schiller's aesthetic treatises had changed from one of disgust to one of enthusiastic approval.

The only reason for mentioning now this growth of interest in aesthetics is the fact that it in turn increased his interest in

---

[22] *The London Magazine*, X (1824), 268. See also *The Life of Friedrich Schiller*, edited by H. D. Traill (London, 1899), p. 198.

[23] *Two Note Books*, 41, 42-45.   [24] *The London Magazine*, X, 22.

[25] *The Life of Friedrich Schiller*, pp. 113-114, 200-201, 320, and *The Love Letters*, II, 31, 48, 105.

transcendental philosophy. Schiller himself had stated that his work *Über die Ästhetische Erziehung des Menschen* was founded "chiefly upon Kantian principles." [26] And since this *Aesthetic Letters* was Carlyle's favorite among Schiller's aesthetic treatises, he was of course aware of Schiller's statement of indebtedness. Indeed, in the last part of the magazine version of Carlyle's Biography of Schiller, finished in February, 1824, he dealt although in brief fashion, with the influence of Kant on Schiller. He deplored this influence as the cause of obscure terminology and of greater difficulty than belonged intrinsically to the subjects discussed in the essays. Although he charged Kant's philosophy in general with obscurity and emptiness, he stated his reluctance to discuss this topic because his acquaintance with it was only a very limited one. And he urged the need of more knowledge about the system before it was rejected in England.[27] Carlyle himself soon attempted to put into practice this injunction to gain more knowledge. During the summer, shortly after his arrival in London, he visited Coleridge at Highgate. And in a narrow place in the garden walk, when he had the oracle to himself, he " tried hard to get something about *Kant* and Co. from him, about 'reason' *versus* 'understanding,' and the like; but in vain. . . ." [28] Whether or not Crabb Robinson gave him any aid on this problem, it is impossible to say. But by January 31, 1825, when Carlyle finished the book version of *The Life of Schiller,* he showed more interest in Kant than he had shown while he was occupied with the earlier version. However, he was still cautious.

The Philosophy of Kant is probably combined with errors to its very core; but perhaps also, this ponderous unmanageable dross may bear in it the everlasting gold of truth! Mighty spirits have already laboured in refining it: is it wise in us to take up with the base pewter of Utility, and renounce such projects altogether? We trust, not.

And to this passage he attached a footnote containing the question, "Are our hopes from Mr. Coleridge always to be fruitless?" [29]

[26] Friedrich Schiller, *The Works of Friedrich Schiller. Aesthetical and Philosophical Essays*, edited by Haskell Dole (N. Y., 1902), I, 4.

[27] *The London Magazine*, X, 21-22.

[28] *Reminiscences*, II, 131-132. He probably made this visit before June 23, 1824: Froude's *Thomas Carlyle . . . 1795-1835*, I, 179, and *The Love Letters*, I, 379.

[29] *The Life of Friedrich Schiller*, p. 114.

Probably this question reflected the disappointment that he had felt in his visit to Highgate. By the time of his departure from London he seems to have learned little more of German philosophy than he had known when he went there. But at last he was interested in the subject. And he had at least made an effort to gain insight into the Kantian conception of reason.

The task of preparing the volumes known as *German Romance,* which Carlyle undertook as soon as he returned to Scotland, left him no time to develop his philosophic interest further. Therefore, it was not until the completion of this work that he turned again to his interest in Kant. On September 27, 1826, he had arrived at the 150th page of Kant's *Kritik der reinen Vernunft,*— not only reading it, he said, but partially understanding it.[30] It is not proved that he ever went farther than this point in the actual reading of Kant's works.[31] But before the year was out, he had somehow acquired a distinction between reason and understanding. An entry in his notebook, written in December, illustrates this distinction:

[30] *The Love Letters,* II, 324.

[31] At some time during the next spring, 1827, he stated that he had read only 100 pages of Kant (*Two Note Books,* p. 113). Whether he actually had read 150 pages or 100 pages, the general significance of the statements is the same. That is, he had not resumed his first-hand study of Kant since he had put aside the *Kritik der reinen Vernunft* in confusion during the early fall of 1826. Instead of resuming his direct study of Kant, he continued his approach by the indirect method of using popular interpreters and intermediators. In *PMLA,* L (1935), 807-827, I have suggested two additions to the list of previously known intermediators between Kant and Carlyle. The first of these new sources is Carl Leonhard Reinhold's *Beytrage zur leichtern Übersicht des Zustandes der Philosophie beym Anfange des 19 Jahrhunderts* (Hamburg, 1801-1803, 6v.). Compare Reinhold's *Beytrage,* I, 12-13, 7, 9, 10-11, with Carlyle's *Two Note Books,* p. 100; *Beytrage,* 1, 20, 72-73, 75-76, with *Two Note Books,* 102-103; and *Beytrage,* I, 12-16, 71-72, with Carlyle's *Critical and Miscellaneous Essays,* I, 79-81.

The second of the new sources of Carlyle's information concerning German philosophy is P. A. Stapfer's "Probleme de l'esprit humain," *Revue Encyclopedique,* XXXIII (February, 1827), 414-431. Compare this review article with the statements derived from it and entered on pages 112-113 of Carlyle's *Two Note Books.*

The latest and most complete discussion of Carlyle's early intellectual relations with Germany is Professor Harrold's book *Carlyle and German Thought: 1819-1834.*

—Yes, it is true! the decisions of Reason (Vernunft) are superior to those of Understanding (Verstand): the latter vary in every age (by what laws?), while the former last forever, and are the same in all forms of manhood.[32]

This estimate of reason—that its findings are permanent truth—is, at last, entirely favorable. And it indicates a great change from his old notion that reason was the enemy of man's spiritual peace. Indeed, in his fragmentary autobiographical romance *Wotton Reinfred,* the character Wotten discovered that intellectual culture could be combined with moral results. At least it was so in the circle surrounding Dalbrook:

Men equally informed and cultivated he [Wotton] had sometimes met with, but seldom or never had he seen such culture of the intellect combined with such moral results, nay, as it appeared, conducing to them.[33]

Intellectual culture, then, might actually conduce to moral results. Furthermore, the study of a popular book by Fichte and one by Schelling had a strong influence upon Carlyle. So great was his change of attitude toward reason by late 1827 that, in "The State of German Literature," he discussed with evident approval what he believed was a Kantian conception of that faculty. Kantists, he said, considered reason "the highest faculty in man," and believed that it dominated "that holier region, where Poetry, and Virtue and Divinity abide." [34] His interest in the practical results of German thought seems to have been still further increased by his study of Novalis.[35] And in the essay written on Novalis at the beginning of 1829, he gave his most explicit discussion of the transcendental philosophy. The transcendentalists, said Carlyle, recognize in

---

[32] *Two Note Books,* 83-84. By June 4, 1827, the character Dalbrook, representing Carlyle's attempt to assume a Kantian viewpoint, re-stated this same distinction between Reason and Understanding in *Wotton Reinfred.* See Thomas Carlyle, *The Last Words of Thomas Carlyle* (London, 1892), p. 63. For date at which writing on the novel *Wotton Reinfred* was discontinued, see *Letters of Thomas Carlyle: 1826-1836,* edited by C. E. Norton (London, 1889), pp. 45-46; see also D. A. Wilson, *Carlyle to the French Revolution (1826-1837)* (London, 1924), p. 24.

[33] *The Last Words of Thomas Carlyle,* p. 59.

[34] *Essays,* I, 83.

[35] For Carlyle's relation to Novalis, see C. F. Harrold, "Carlyle and Novalis," *SP,* XXVII (1930), 47-63.

Reason (*Vernunft*), the pure, ultimate light of our nature; wherein, as they assert, lies the foundation of all Poetry, Virtue, Religion; . . . [G]enerally all true Christian Faith and Devotion, appear, so far as we can see, more or less included in this doctrine of the Transcendentalists; under their several shapes, the essence of them . . . being what is here designated by the name Reason. . . .[36]

It is now a well known fact that Carlyle's understanding of the philosophy of Kant and of his successors was both inadequate and inaccurate.[37] In the passage just quoted Carlyle was stating his own pseudo-critical conception of reason. Reason, in his mind, had taken over and united the desirable traits implied in the old terms *head* and *heart*. And reason seemed to him the foundation of poetry and religion.

Thus far in our discussion the following points have been presented. After a distrust of reason that lasted for several years, Carlyle in 1822 caught a glimpse of the progressive nature of man's successive approximations to truth. Thereupon he began to examine more closely the province of reason, the intellectual faculty that furnished humanity with these successive approximations. By early 1824 he stated his approval of Schiller's unqualified dismissal of dogma that failed to satisfy the rational side of his nature. Moreover, from the study of German aesthetics, especially the aesthetic treatises by Schiller, Carlyle gradually conceived an interest in the new German philosophy. But not until late 1826 did he make a first-hand study of Kant. That study probably was limited to one hundred and fifty pages.[37a] But with the aid of several popular discussions of German philosophy he soon presented in his own writings a distinction between *Vernunft* and *Verstand*. And in the essay on Novalis in 1829, he gave his fullest discussion of the significance of transcendental philosophy. In this essay he stated his own trust in reason as the essence of "all true Christian Faith and Devotion." Thus, inadequate and inaccurate though Carlyle's understanding of Kant and his suc-

[36] *Essays*, II, 27.

[37] Several recent discussions of Carlyle's relations to German philosophy have already been mentioned at the beginning of this paper. The most complete is Professor Harrold's *Carlyle and German Thought*. On the comparison of Carlyle's Reason with the Reason of Kant, Fichte, and Schelling, see especially pp. 131 and 145.

[37a] See above footnote 31.

cessors was, German philosophy seemed to unite for him the desirable traits implied in the old terms *head* and *heart*. The old problem seemed solved. And reason, re-defined to accommodate his conception of *Vernunft,* appeared to him the foundation and unifier of poetry and religion.

II. Tolerance

The principle of intellectual tolerance with opinions and facts that do not conform to the bounds of conventional dogma and morality is frequently a part of the rational cast of mind. Although Carlyle cannot be said ever to have possessed a strictly rational cast of mind, at least his early attitude of distrust and hostility toward reason underwent a diametric change before 1829. And, along with this change, he developed and enunciated a principle of tolerance.

It was early in 1822, as has been shown, that his distrust of reason was given full expression. And it is logical that, with this early distrust of intellect, he should have shown an intolerant attitude toward the intellectual force that attempted to overthrow theological and moral boundaries. Indeed, in January, 1822, he was intolerant enough to denounce Faust's intellectual activity as criminal. The criminality began, he thought, when Faust allowed his mind to wander—even in search of truth—until it doubted the existence of a providence and the foundation of moral distinctions.[38] But Carlyle was condemning himself in the same sentence with Faust, for his own faith in established theological dogma had broken down some four or five years before this essay on *Faust* was written. And rather than content himself with his own sentence of damnation, he sought further.

His half-guesses in the spring of 1822 have already been noticed. He supposed that truth *immer wird, nie ist,* and that the art of reasoning comes and goes and changes its fashions like clothes. As has been pointed out, this notion is closely related to the eighteenth century idea of progress. If this notion of the progressive development of truth is pursued logically, it will eventually involve the principle of tolerance for the various approximations

---

[38] *Essay on Goethe's Faust*, pp. 42-43. The passage has already been quoted at length in the preceding section of this paper.

to truth. That is, in the terminology of *Sartor Resartus*, it will involve tolerance for the changing clothes that truth wears in different epochs and in different minds. But in 1822 Carlyle was not sure that truth ought to change its clothes. Perhaps the established form was the better one, after all. His uncertainty appeared in the notebook entry of April 13, 1822, on Thomas Ellwood. Carlyle believed that this Quaker had attained to victorious life because he had relied unquestioningly upon his religious creed as his support, his all in all. And this statement about Ellwood's faith gave rise to a speculation as to whether it was best, as a general principle, for men to hold to the old tried way. He wondered whether it was better for men to have *a* straight road—even though a false one—formed for them through the confusion of life, or for men to spend their lives searching for a true road without any preassurance that they would discover it. But he could not yet answer this problem of the century as to whether the old dogma or the new struggle availed most for the way of the soul. All he could do was to insist that the choice be made only after a comparison of the weak and faithful Ellwood with such strong and rational men as Alfieri, Goethe, and Voltaire. And he closed this important passage with the query: What *is* the proper province of reason?[39] As Carlyle put the question concerning faithful Ellwood and rational Alfieri, Goethe, and Voltaire, any decision in favor of reason would necessarily have carried with it tolerance for an unorthodox religious faith. Although he was not yet prepared to make this decision in favor of reason and tolerance, it is clear that the strong advocates of reason had made a great impression on his mind.

The year from 1823 to 1824, spent in intermittent preparation of the serial biography of Schiller, was an important period in the development of Carlyle's principle of tolerance. A notebook entry of March, 1823, shows his growing trust in tolerance, at the same time that it shows his growing trust in Goethe. Carlyle thought that Goethe's tolerance toward the critical philosophy in Germany was wiser than the hate and denunciation aimed at it by Herder and Wieland. In spite of Carlyle's belief that "the new philosophy was driving fiercely butting like a wild Bull against the ortho-

[39] *Two Note Books*, p. 22. The passage has already been quoted at length in the preceding section.

dox creed of Germany," he considered Goethe right. Goethe " was clear for ' letting it have its time as everything has.' This was right, old Goethe, and I respect thee for the solid judgment of this saying." [40]   And, as has been shown, in the final section of the serial biography of Schiller, which was finished in February, 1824, Carlyle praised Schiller's intellectual honesty.[41]   Here was the answer to the problem that Carlyle had left unsettled when it had arisen in April, 1822, in connection with Ellwood. Now, in connection with the German poet, he had reached his decision in favor of reason. Schiller was to be commended in freeing himself from any belief, however dear, if it proved false. This is the working of the principle of tolerance with respect to the overthrow of religious dogma. Already, by 1824, Carlyle's acceptance of the principle of tolerance was under way.

The several pieces of evidence that have just been recalled from the section of this discussion that deals with reason, illustrate the close relationship thus far between reason and tolerance in Carlyle's mind. Much more of the evidence on the development of tolerance is exactly the same as that already presented in tracing the development of Carlyle's favorable attitude toward reason. And the interpretation of this evidence with respect to tolerance is so obvious that it is not necessary to re-examine and re-present the details in this section. In summary, it will suffice to say that, while the faculty of reason was becoming triumphant in his estimation and was forming a temporary union of poetry and religion, tolerance became one of his fundamental principles.

---

[40] *Two Note Books*, p. 46. Carlyle was too much attracted to Goethe that in the spring of 1823 he undertook the translation of *Meister's Lehr-jahre* (*Early Letters of Thomas Carlyle*, II, 199-200; and *The Love Letters*, I, 216). But the path of tolerance—tolerance even for Goethe's opinions— did not run smooth. Sometimes Carlyle's anti-stage Puritanism got the better of tolerance. And when he read of Meister's players and libidinous actresses, with their sorry pasteboard apparatus for beautifying and enlivening the ' Moral World,' he admitted that his own feelings became as mild and charitable as those of a starving hyaena (*Early Letters of Thomas Carlyle*, II, 223-224: September 21, 1823). Although Carlyle refused to take moral responsibility for what Goethe had written, he said in his preface to the translation, that he had expurgated less than a page from the original (*Wilhelm Meister's Apprenticeship and Travels* (London, 1907), I, 10. See also *The Love Letters*, I, 339-340).

[41] *The London Magazine*, X, 268.

A few passages chosen from Carlyle's writings during the years from 1826 to 1829 will amply illustrate his principle of tolerance. In the first of these passages, which occurs in *German Romance,* he requested a mild judgment for the erring Hoffmann.

Let us not forget, that for a mind like his the path of propriety was difficult to find, still more difficult to keep. Moody, sensitive and fantastic, he wandered through the world like a foreign presence, subject to influences of which common natures have happily no glimpse.[42]

Toward the end of the same year, December, 1826, he mentioned in his notebook the misfortune of a close-minded intolerance of new thought:

Few men have the secret of being at once determinate (*bestimmt*) and open; of knowing what they do know, and yet lying ready for farther knowledge.[43]

Late the next year he again sounded the note of tolerance in a passage on Zacharias Werner's religious experience.

Above all, there are mysteries and unsounded abysses in every human heart; and that is but a questionable philosophy which undertakes so readily to explain them. Religious belief especially, at least when it seems heartfelt and well-intentioned, is no subject for harsh or even irreverent investigation. He is a wise man that, having such a belief, knows and sees clearly the grounds of it in himself: and those, we imagine, who have explored with strictest scrutiny the secret of their own bosoms will be least apt to rush with intolerant violence into that of other men's.[44]

But perhaps the clearest statement of Carlyle's principle of tolerance is found in the essay on Burns, which was finished at Craigenputtock in September, 1828.[45]

. . . the world is habitually unjust in its judgment of such men [as Burns]; unjust on many grounds, of which this one may be stated as the substance: It decides, like a court of law, by dead statutes; and not positively but negatively, less on what is done right, than on what is or is not done wrong. Not the few inches of deflection from the mathematical orbit, which are so easily measured, but the *ratio* of these to the whole diameter, constitutes the real aberration. This orbit may be a planet's, its diameter the breadth of the solar system; or it may be a city hippo-

---

[42] *German Romance,* edited by H. D. Traill (London, 1898), II, 18.
[43] *Two Note Books,* pp. 77-78.
[44] *Essays,* I, 145. The essay on Werner was finished by November 25, 1827: see *Letters of Thomas Carlyle,* p. 79.
[45] *Two Note Books,* p. 129.

drome; nay, the circle of a ginhorse, its diameter a score of feet or paces. But the inches of deflection only are measured. . . . Here lies the root of many a blind, cruel condemnation of Burnses, Swifts, Rousseaus, which one never listens to with approval.[46]

Here, then, is a calculus for determining the worth of a strong individual who breaks over the bounds of conventional morality. By it, he could have compared "Ellwood, a weak man, with Alfieri, Goethe, Voltaire, strong men," and could have awarded the palm without hesitation.[47]

This second section of our discussion shows that, along with Carlyle's changing attitude toward reason, he developed the principle of tolerance. He believed that the course of morality varied as individuals varied. Therefore he condemned the practice of judging men negatively, by the amount of their deflection from the course of conventional propriety. Instead, he urged the positive and tolerant principle, first, of understanding each individual's potential course; second, of measuring the individual's deflection from this course; and finally, of calculating the ratio between the potentiality and the performance. "Not the few inches of deflection from the mathematical orbit, . . . but the *ratio* of these to the whole diameter, constitutes the real aberration." This is Carlyle's principle of tolerance, stated in September, 1828. And this principle of tolerance, characteristic of progressives, had become deeply interwoven with other lines of his thought.

III. THE CONFLICT BETWEEN RELIGION AND POETRY

As has been shown, Carlyle's approval of reason and his approval of tolerance developed together under German influence and interacted with each other in a tendency to exalt poetry and the poet. However, as will be shown, his own natural leanings with respect to religion could at times prove strong enough to qualify his merely aesthetic or humane judgments. Thus, for years, his intellectual

---

[46] *Essays*, I, 317-318. A similar idea occurs at the end of Burns's own poem, "Address to the Unco Guid."

[47] In fact, in March, 1829, he did discuss the last of these men, Voltaire (see *Essays*, I, 396-468). But in this man, whom posterity frequently considers a Promethean, Carlyle found little that he considered truly great (see for example, pp. 414, 446, 454-456). Nevertheless, he insisted, even in this essay, on tolerance as a principle (see p. 467).

development was swayed by the conflict between his native Puritanism and his acquired romanticism. It has been seen that a redefinition of reason brought peace for a while. It remains to be seen that the application of the principle of tolerance throws new light on the issue between poetry and religion and indicates where the larger conflict lay.

Early in his study of German literature, Carlyle came in contact with the notion that the beautiful is higher than the good,—that aesthetic culture is superior to moral culture. And at first he disapproved. For instance, in March, 1823, at the beginning of his preparation for the biography of Schiller, he made the following long note on the subject:

The pursuit of the Beautiful, the representing of it in suitable forms, and the diffusion of the feelings arising from it, operated as a kind of religion in his soul. He talks in some of his essays about the *Aesthetic's* being a *necessary* means of improvement among political societies: his efforts in this cause accordingly not only satisfied the restless activity, the desire of creating and working upon others, which forms the great want of an elevated mind, but yielded a sort of balsam to his *conscience;* he viewed himself as an Apostle of the sublime. Pity that he had no better way of satisfying it! A play-house shews but indifferently as an arena for the Moralist: it is even inferior to the synod of the theologian. One is tired to death with his and Goethe's *palabra* about the nature of the fine arts. Did Shakespeare know aught of the *aesthetic?* Did Homer? [48]

Though at first he disapproved of the play-house as an arena for the moralist, this disapproval was not permanent. There was a new tone in a passage written by the end of February, 1824, in the Third Part of the magazine version of this biography.

Literature was his [Schiller's] creed, the dictate of his conscience; he was the Apostle of the Sublime and Beautiful, and this his calling made a hero of him. [49]

And in the preface to *Wilhelm Meister's Apprenticeship*, which was written in May, 1824, he stated his belief that artistic beauty " has its foundation in the deepest nature of man. . . ." [50]   At the

---

[48] *Two Note Books*, p. 41.

[49] *The London Magazine*, X, 268-269.

[50] J. W. Goethe, *Wilhelm Meister's Apprenticeship and Travels* (Translated by Carlyle), I, 8.

beginning of the next year, 1825, he completed his revision of *The Life of Schiller* preparatory to its publication as a book.   One of the most striking additions that he made was a discussion of Schiller's *Letters on the Aesthetic Culture of Man*.   He believed that the laws of criticism discussed in Schiller's aesthetic essays were derived from the inmost nature of man.[51]

These *Letters on Aesthetic Culture,* without the aid of anything which the most sceptical could designate as superstition, trace out and attempt to sanction for us a system of morality, in which the sublimest feelings of the Stoic and the Christian are represented but as stages in our progress to the pinnacle of true human grandeur . . . [52]

And near the end of the book he was even more specific.

As Schiller viewed it, genuine Literature includes the essence of philosophy, religion, art; whatever speaks to the immortal part of man. . . . The treasures of Literature are thus celestial, imperishable, beyond all price: with her is the shrine of our best hopes, the palladium of pure manhood; to be among the guardians and servants of this is the noblest function that can be intrusted to a mortal.[53]

Furthermore, in a passage written about Tieck in *German Romance,* there occurs a similar thought.   "Tieck's mind," Carlyle believed, "all Goodness, all that was noble or excellent in Nature . . . combined itself under the image of Poetic Beauty. . . ."[54] But these suggestions that art includes religion—if they are to be thus construed—dealt more with the views of Schiller and Tieck than with the views of Carlyle himself.

During March, 1826, in the same book that contained the passage just quoted concerning Tieck, Carlyle made a positive statement of his own.   This statement occurred in the biographical sketch of Goethe.

The angels and demons that can lay prostrate our hearts in the nineteenth century must be of another and more cunning fashion than those that subdued us in the ninth.   To have attempted, to have begun this enterprise, may be accounted the greatest praise.   That Goethe ever meditated it, in the form here set forth, we have no direct evidence: but indeed such is the end and aim of high poetry at all times and seasons; for the fiction of the poet is not falsehood, but the purest truth; and if he would lead

---

[51] *The Life of Friedrich Schiller,* p. 113.
[52] *Ibid.,* p. 114.
[53] *Ibid.,* pp. 200-201.
[54] *German Romance,* I, 258.

captive our whole being, not rest satisfied with a part of it, he must address us on interests that *are*, not *were*, ours; and in a dialect which finds a response, and not a contradiction, within our bosoms.[55]

Although this passage refers to poetic fiction as the purest truth, and may even suggest Carlyle's preference for a poetic statement of truth rather than a religious statement, he did not base his preference on purely aesthetic grounds. Indeed he scorned the kind of art that aimed at only aesthetic pleasure.

> It is a damnable heresy in criticism to maintain either expressly or implicitly that the ultimate object of Poetry is sensation. That of Cookery is such, but not that of Poetry.[56]

Instead of mere pleasure, he believed that the aim of all literature was some variety of instruction.[57] For example, about the end of 1826, after he had written the first of the " Pilpay Junior " fables, he entered this thought in his notebook:

> The instruction communicated by Fable is in its nature chiefly *prohibitive*; therefore not the highest species, which latter belongs to the Province of Poetry. (?) [58]

Apparently he believed that the highest type of instruction, or perhaps of truth, was communicated by poetry.

This didactic notion of literature was reinforced by his study of Fichte in 1827. And in " The State of German Literature," which was finished in October, he re-stated thus an idea from Fichte's *Über das Wesen des Gelehrten*:

> Literary Men are the appointed interpreters of this Divine Idea [which pervades the universe]; a perpetual priesthood . . . standing forth, generation after generation, as the dispensers and living types of God's everlasting wisdom, to show it in their writings and actions, in such particular form as their own particular times require it in. For each age, by the law

---

[55] Goethe, *Wilhelm Meister's Apprenticeship and Travels* (Translated by Carlyle), I, 29.

[56] *Two Note Books*, p. 71: December 3, 1826. See also *The Last Words of Thomas Carlyle*, pp. 95-96.

[57] Professor Roe believes that didacticism is " an element by no means implied in Carlyle's critical principles and not much evident in his earlier criticism." (*Carlyle as a Critic of Literature*, p. 101.) Clearly enough, Carlyle's didacticism increased, but it also seems to have played a part in his thought even as early as 1826.

[58] *Two Note Books*, p. 92.

of its nature, is different from every other age, and demands a different representation of the Divine Idea, the essence of which is the same in all; so that the literary man of one century is only by mediation and reinterpretation applicable to the wants of another.[59]

This passage contains in it some of the most important ideas that influenced Carlyle's thought. His notion of the hero is largely derived from this *Über das Wesen des Gelehrten*.[60] The "appointed interpreters" of the Divine Idea are kin to the Calvinistic Elect.[61] A perpetual literary priesthood dispensing everlasting wisdom in forms appropriate to the times, resembles Schiller's conception that the poet is a purifier of his age, who, through the instrumentality of art, may restore man's lost dignity to him.[62] And the last sentence in the quotation recalls the idea of progress, which had become a part of Carlyle's thought: "each age . . . is different . . . , and demands a different representation of the Divine Idea, the essence of which is the same in all. . . ." Thus in 1827 these four ideas converged on the man of letters. And in Carlyle's estimation, this convergence gave to the man of letters an importance that he never lost.

If, as Carlyle understood from Fichte, literary men were the special interpreters of divine wisdom in forms that changed to fit the changing times, might not the greatest poet of the age present through his art a finer view of morality than that familiar through nursery tales? Whether or not such a logical question was in

---

[59] *Essays*, I, 58-59.

[60] Lehman, *Carlyle's Theory of the Hero*, pp. 108-122.

[61] Flügel, Thomas Carlyle's *Religiöse und sittliche Entwicklung und Weltanschauung*, p. 142.

[62] Schiller, *Aesthetical and Philosophical Essays* (Translated by Haskell Dole), I, 30-31. Lehman (*Carlyle's Theory of the Hero*, pp. 67-68) points out the relationship between the notions of Fichte, Schiller, and Carlyle. Milton too may have played a part in this conception of the poet-priest. On April 22, 1822, Carlyle finished reading "The Reason of Church Government Urged against Prelaty" (*Two Note Books*, p. 26). He commented thus on "The Preface" to "The Second Book": "The second book opens with a fine exordium on the Author's own studies and aspirations. . . ." And after over a page of comment on the essay, Carlyle added: "I never saw so eloquent a person. What boundless store of metaphors! What infinitude of thoughts! What strong & continuous fervour of soul!— Upon the whole however I am only beginning to see Milton. . . ." (*Two Note Books*, p. 27.)

Carlyle's mind, a passage written in March, 1828, on Goethe's *Helena* deserves careful attention. It amounts to a reversal of his earlier judgment concerning Faust's criminality.

> Faust . . . cannot be regarded as a wicked, much less as an utterly reprobate man. . . . To send him to the Pit of Woe, to render such a character the eternal slave of Mephistopheles, would look like making darkness triumphant over light, blind force over erring reason; or at best, were cutting the Gordian knot, not loosing it. If we mistake not, Goethe's *Faust* will have a finer moral than the old nursery-tale, or the other plays and tales that have been founded on it. Our seared and blighted yet still noble Faust will not end in the madness of horror, but in Peace grounded on better Knowledge. Whence that Knowledge is to come, what higher and freer world of Art or Religion may be hovering in the mind of the Poet, we will not try to surmise; perhaps in bright aërial emblematic glimpses, he may yet show it us, transient and afar off, yet clear with orient beauty, as a Land of Wonders and new Poetic Heaven." [63]

The publication of the complete drama *Faust* four years later proved that there was some accuracy in Carlyle's predictions. For example, in the completed version, Faust does not end in the madness of horror. Perhaps, as Carlyle suggested, the new end does involve a finer moral than the old end, which consigned Faust to the Pit of Woe. However, in 1828, this poetic morality was only a hint on Carlyle's part. He had not yet investigated the logical implications of this hint. As this paper will show, he was to think and to write much more on the subject of poetic morality. Here he only broached the subject.

In spite of the tendency, already pointed out, to consider art as broader and more inclusive than religion, Carlyle's interpretation of German philosophy soon began to dim the glory of aesthetics. After late 1828 he seemed to drift in a direction opposite to the one thus far observed, and to tend toward a subordination of poetry to religion. But this subordination of poetry to religion was a gradual one. For instance, in the essay on Burns, finished in September, he seemed content to rank poetry with religion and to unite the two. [64] In this unification perhaps he was making use of his conception of Kantian reason as " that holier region, where Poetry, and Virtue, and Divinity abide." [65] In his most complete exposition of German transcendentalism, which was written in January, 1829, in the essay on Novalis, Carlyle's religious interests

---

[63] *Essays*, I, 161-162.   [64] *Ibid.*, I, 314.   [65] *Ibid.*, I, 83.

were still more obtrusive. He again assigned to the transcendentalists the belief that "the foundation of all Poetry, Virtue,
Religion" lay in reason.[66] But he chiefly dwelt upon the relationship between transcendentalism and religion. It seemed to him
that the essence of all true Christian faith and devotion was
included in the transcendentalists' conception of reason.[67] Furthermore, the transcendental conceptions of time and space were
enlisted in the service of religion. "If Time and Space have no
absolute existence, . . . it removes a stumbling-block from the
very threshold of our Theology." [68] This extra emphasis upon religion continued during 1829. In March he believed "Our fathers
were wiser than we, when they said . . . that Religion is 'not of
Sense, but of Faith'; not of Understanding, but of Reason. He
who finds himself without the latter, . . . of the Christian Religion . . . has and can have no knowledge." [69] Since Voltaire
lacked this reason and its implications, his chief significance in
Europe seemed to Carlyle that of "a religious Polemic, . . . a
vehement opponent of the Christian Faith." [70] He looked upon
the age of Voltaire as an experiment to decide "With what degree
of vigour a political system . . . without a God or any recognition
of the godlike in man, can be expected to flourish. . . ." [71] In
August he believed that "the Christian Religion . . . must ever
be regarded as the crowning glory, or rather the life and soul, of
our whole modern culture. . . ." [72] And again, in October, philosophy and poetry were both subordinated to religion when he
praised Richter as a man "in whom Philosophy and Poetry are
not only reconciled, but blended together into a purer essence, into
Religion. . . ." [73] Thus by the end of 1829 Carlyle's preference

---

[66] *Ibid.*, II, 27.   [67] *Essays*, II, 27.

[68] *Ibid.*, II, 26. The main significance of German Philosophy to Carlyle
was the fact that it removed an obstacle from the way of his faith. In a
letter written in 1841 he told Espinasse that the only precious thing in
German philosophy seemed to be the "deliverance from the fatal incubus
of Scotch or French philosophy, with its mechanisms and its Atheisms . . ."
(Francis Espinasse, *Literary Recollections and Sketches* (London, 1893),
p. 59). Late in the same decade he again touched upon the main significance: "Kant . . . taught me that I had a soul as well as a body." (*Ibid.*,
pp. 220-221.)

[69] *Essays*, I, 457-458.   [72] *Ibid.*, II, 70.

[70] *Ibid.*, I, 455.   [73] *Ibid.*, II, 100.

[71] *Ibid.*, I, 462.

for religion over poetry had been stated in a number of passages. But so far, these two grand appeals, poetry and religion, had not come into sharp conflict with each other. Thus far, it had been chiefly a matter of emphasis.

Although he had subordinated poetry to religion in 1829, Carlyle clung to the grand idea of the literary calling that had been fostered by his reading of Fichte. And as his social interests grew, he began to apply his own modifications of Fichte's ideal learned man in the English actualities of his own time. In " The Signs of the Times " he stated his trust in journalistic literature as the proper guide of society. He believed that the clergy were being more and more superseded by the journalists.

At no former era has Literature, the printed communication of Thought, been of such importance as it is now. We often hear that the Church is in danger; and truly so it is,—in a danger it seems not to know of: for, with its tithes in the most perfect safety, its functions are becoming more and more superseded. The true Church of England, at this moment, lies in the Editors of its Newspapers. These preach to people daily, weekly; admonishing kings themselves; advising peace or war, with an authority which only the first Reformers, and a long-past class of Popes, were possessed of; inflicting moral censure; imparting moral encouragement, consolation, edification; in all ways diligently ' administering the Discipline of the Church.' [74]

In this quotation the grounds of the conflict between literature and religion become more apparent. Sometimes, when Carlyle centered his attention on the need for social guidance, literature seemed to him the true Church of England. But sometimes, as we have seen, when his attention was more exalted, he considered religion the culmination of all human activity.

His writings on religion as the culmination of art and philosophy continued, for a while. And he was apparently unhampered by the arrival of a new German book reiterating the doctrine that art is superior to both philosophy and religion. While he was at work on the Richter essay, about the middle of October, 1829, the first two volumes of the correspondence between Schiller and Goethe reached him in a packet that had been dispatched from Goethe during the summer.[75] By November 3 he had already read

[74] *Essays*, II, 77.

[75] *Correspondence between Goethe and Carlyle*, pp. 139-140, 146, 155, 159. The full title of the work was *Briefwechsel zwischen Schiller und Goethe*

this part of the correspondence once and was proposing to read it a second time, and to use it as a point of departure for a new essay on Schiller.[76]

Apparently he set about the second reading immediately, for the essay " Schiller " itself was finished by December 22.[77] In the essay he quoted from Schiller's letters two passages indicative of the poet's views on the question that Carlyle believed "the highest of all philosophic questions." In both of these passages, Schiller was discussing Goethe's *Wilhelm Meister*. Obviously the important thing to Carlyle was the fact that these passages dealt pointedly with the relation between art and religion. Schiller had written as follows:

If you study the specific character of Christianity, what distinguishes it from all monotheistic Religions, it lies in nothing else than in that *making-dead of the Law*, the removal of that Kantean Imperative, instead of which Christianity requires a free Inclination. It is thus, in its pure form, a representing of Moral Beauty, or the Incarnation of the Holy; and in this sense, the only *aesthetic* Religion: hence, too, I explain to myself why it so prospers with female natures, and only in women is now to be met with under a tolerable figure.[78]

In this first passage, Schiller considered the aesthetic element the distinguishing characteristic of the Christian religion. On the same page of the essay Carlyle presented the other passage from Schiller.

Within the aesthetic temper there arises no want of those grounds of comfort, which are to be drawn from speculation: such a temper has self-subsistence, has infinitude, within itself; only when the Sensual and the Moral in man strive hostilely together, need help be sought of pure Reason. A healthy poetic nature wants, as you yourself say, no Moral Law, no Rights of Man, no Political Metaphysics. You might have added as well, it wants no Deity, no Immortality, to stay and uphold itself withal. Those three points round which, in the long-run, all speculation turns, may in truth afford such a nature matter for poetic play, but can never become serious concerns and necessities for it.[79]

---

in den Jahren 1794 bis 1804 (Stuttgart u. Tübingen: 1828-1829, 6v.). Carlyle had only the first two volumes of it at this time: See *Correspondence between Goethe and Carlyle*, p. 172.

[76] *Ibid.*, p. 155.   [77] *Ibid.*, pp. 161-162.

[78] Carlyle's translation occurs in *Essays*, II, 213. The original passage occurs in *Briefwechsel zwischen Schiller und Goethe*, I, 195.

[79] Carlyle's translation occurs in *Essays*, II, 213; the original passage in *Briefwechsel*, II, 131.

In this second passage Schiller extended his argument to say that, since the healthy aesthetic temperament included infinitude within itself, it consequently did not need such aids as philosophy or religious faith might furnish. In the two passages, taken together as Carlyle presented them, Schiller was saying that Christianity in its purest form borrows its distinguishing characteristic from the aesthetic realm; whereas, on the other hand, the healthy aesthetic temperament is entirely independent of religion. He was making a sharp contrast between art and religion. And to him the advantage lay very decidedly on the side of art. Moreover, Carlyle's comment on the second passage makes it clear that he understood the import of Schiller's reasoning:

This last seems a singular opinion; and may prove, if it be correct, that Schiller himself was no 'healthy poetic nature'; for undoubtedly with him those three points were 'serious concerns and necessities'; as many portions of his work, and various entire treatises, will testify. Nevertheless, it plays an important part in his theories of Poetry; and often, under milder forms, returns on us there.[80]

But Carlyle's comment showed little excitement over the new statement of Schiller's notion. And at this time he entered into no special pleading for or against it.

Although later developments will show that this notion of art-over-religion had a deep influence, Carlyle's reaction to it during the next few months seems to have been negative. That is, in spite of Schiller's dictum, Carlyle continued for a while to consider religion superior to art. Some passages from the private notebook will show, better than the published writings do, how his mind was working in the spring of 1830.

I have now almost done with the Germans. Having seized their opinions, I must turn me to inquire *how* true are they? That truth is in them, no lover of Truth will doubt: but how much? And after all, one needs an intellectual Scheme (or ground plan of the Universe) drawn with one's own instruments.—

I think I have got rid of Materialism: Matter no longer seems to me so ancient, so unsubduable, so *certain* and palpable as Mind. *I* am Mind: whether matter or not I know not—and care not.—Mighty glimpses into the spiritual Universe I have sometimes had (about the true nature of Religion, the possibility, after all, of 'supernatural' (really natural)

---

[80] *Essays*, II, 213.

influences &c. &c.) : would they could but stay with me, and ripen into a perfect view!

—Miracle? What is a Miracle? Can there be a thing more miraculous than any other thing? I myself am a standing wonder. It is 'the inspiration of the Almighty that giveth us understanding.'—

What is Poetry? Do I really love Poetry? I sometimes fancy almost, not. The jingle of maudlin persons, with their mere (even genuine) 'sensibility' is unspeakably fatiguing to me. My greatly most delightful reading is, where some Goethe musically *teaches* me. Nay, *any* fact, relating especially to man, is still valuable and pleasing.— [81]

In other words, Carlyle had derived from his superficial study of transcendental philosophy, a viewpoint that abolished materialism from his mind.[82] Now he turned away from German philosophy to perfect his own spiritualistic conception of the universe. Already he had had "Mighty glimpses into the spiritual Universe"; the natural sometimes seemed to him a revelation of the supernatural; he sometimes conceived actual human history as the revelation of Divinity. And in comparison with awe-inspiring fact, sentimental and fictional poetry seemed tawdry. He doubted that he had a real love for poetry. Carlyle had reached this point in his thinking during the spring of 1830. It is one of the little ironies of his life that, at this very time, he was engaged in writing a history of German literature. And although the moralistic and religious strain of his nature was pressing poetry thin, he persevered in his self-appointed literary task until midsummer.

In 1830 he tried hard to understand morality and religion, and to estimate their importance in human history. Schiller's dictum that art was superior to religion and philosophy stimulated his speculation. On his own part, he had tended to exalt religion above the other two interests. Philosophy had served him chiefly as a remover of an obstacle from the way of religious faith. And now that the obstacle was removed, he could even fall back occasionally on his old conception of an opposition between intellect and morals, to justify this subordination of philosophy to religion. For example, in September, after a passage in which he contrasted Aristotle's philosophy and the Sermon on the Mount, he stated this conclusion:

[81] *Two Note Books*, pp. 150-151.
[82] See also Espinasse, *Literary Recollections and Sketches*, pp. 39, 220-221.

One thing we see: the moral nature of man is deeper than his intellectual; things planted down in the former may grow as if forever; the latter as a kind of drift mould produces only annuals. What is Jesus Christ's significance? *Altogether moral.*[83]

But this opposition between intellect and morality was occasional.[84] His chief difficulty at this time was not the relation between philosophy and religion. It was, rather, the relation between art and religion. On the same page that contained the passage just quoted, he asked himself what was the moral significance of the artists Schiller and Goethe. And at the end of December he asked a still more pointed question:

> What *is* Art and Poetry? Is the Beautiful really higher than the Good? A higher *form* thereof? Thus were the Poet not only a Priest but a High-priest.[85]

In this passage, written at the end of 1830, Carlyle was still far from Schiller's viewpoint. But at least he had put the important question: " Is the Beautiful really higher than the Good? " And his attempts at an answer were forthcoming.

By the beginning of 1831 this question of the relative values of the beautiful and the good had become a pressing one. Perhaps a contributory element in the situation is the fact that he was then resuming work on *Sartor Resartus,* his chief art production.[86] Whatever the reason, in February he again stated the problem of the relative values.

> On the whole I wish I could define to myself the true relation of moral genius to poetic genius; of Religion and Poetry. Are they one and the same, different forms of the same; and if so which is to stand higher, the Beautiful or the Good? Schiller and Goethe seem to say the former, as if it included the latter and might supersede it: how truly I can never

---

[83] *Two Note Books,* p. 171.

[84] See *Two Note Books,* p. 277 (May 16, 1832) and *Essays,* II, 436-437 (about July 1832), where intellect and morality seem to be unified. But, on the other hand, see *Essays,* IV, 148.

[85] *Two Note Books,* p. 180.

[86] On January 21, 1831, he recalled from London the first version of the work that he had finished on October 28, 1830, and named " Thoughts on Clothes." He was preparing to add more biography and a section on society and one on religion. The final product, *Sartor Resartus,* was finished by August 4, 1831. See *Letters of Thomas Carlyle,* p. 183 and *Two Note Books,* pp. 177 and 183.

well see.—Meanwhile that the *faculties* always go together seems clear.
It is a gross calumny on human nature to say that there ever was a
mind of surpassing talent that did not also surpass in *capability* of
virtue; and *vice versa*; nevertheless in both cases there are 'female
geniuses' too, minds that admire and receive, but can hardly create; I have
observed in these also the taste for Religion and for Poetry go together.
The most wonderful words that I ever heard of being uttered by man are
those in the four Evangelists, by Jesus of Nazareth. Their intellectual
talent is hardly inferior to their moral. On this subject, if I live, I hope
to have much to say.[87]

In *Sartor Resartus,* finished in the same year, 1831, he did have
much to say on this subject of the coexistence of the artist and
the prophet in the same person. For instance, Teufelsdröckh dealt
with it in his chapter on symbols:

Highest of all Symbols are those wherein the Artist or Poet has risen into
Prophet, and all men can recognize a present God, and worship the same:
I mean religious Symbols.[88]

This and various other passages in *Sartor Resartus* suggest that in
the summer of 1831 Carlyle still considered religion a higher manifestation than poetry.[89]

But either the working-out of *Sartor Resartus* or the preliminary
speculation that grew into the essay " Characteristics " seems to
have shed some new light upon the problem of the relative values
of religion and art. Apparently he found additional evidence that
literature was better able than the church to lead society through
the cataclysmic changes that he foresaw and bring it to a successful palingenesis.[90] And a notebook entry of October 10, which
will repay careful consideration, showed a much clearer view of
his old problem of art and religion than do any of his earlier statements. Moreover, it showed a clear view of the decisive principle,
tolerance, upon which, logically, the problem turned. This entry,
like the one written in February on the same subject, began with a
reference to Goethe and Schiller.

When Goethe and Schiller say or insinuate that Art is higher than
Religion, do they mean perhaps this: That whereas Religion represents
(what is the essence of Truth for men) the Good as *infinitely* (the word

---

[87] *Two Note Books*, pp. 188-189.
[88] *Sartor Resartus*, p. 203.
[89] *Ibid.*, pp. 194, 195-196.
[90] See *Sartor Resartus*, pp. 196 and 230, and *Essays*, III, 23.

is emphatic) different from the Evil, but sets them in a state of *hostility* (as in Heaven and Hell),—Art likewise admits and inculcates this quite infinite difference; but *without* hostility, with peacefulness; like the difference of two Poles which cannot coalesce, yet do not quarrel, nay should not quarrel for both are essential to the whole? In this way is Goethe's morality to be conidered as a *higher* (apart from its comprehensiveness, nay universality) than has hitherto been promulgated?—*Sehr einseitig*! Yet perhaps there is a glimpse of the truth here.[91]

In this new statement of the old problem concerning art and religion, attention was focused upon the dualistic elements, good and evil, in man's life. These elements were characterized as being by their natures diametrically opposed to each other. And two views were stated concerning the relationship between these constitutionally opposed elements. Religion was represented as stipulating a hostile relationship; whereas art was represented as stipulating a peaceful relationship. Ultimately, any decision given on the proposition thus stated would turn on the point of tolerance. That is, on the one hand, the opposed elements of good and evil in human life would be conceived as hostile and intolerent toward one another; and religion would gain the decision. Or, on the other hand, the opposed elements of good and evil would be conceived as without hostility, peaceful, and tolerant toward one another; and art would gain the decision. In the quotation under consideration Carlyle gave a hesitating preference to the latter of the alternatives. This preference chose tolerance instead of intolerance,—apparently chose art instead of religion. In making this choice, when the question was put in this fashion, he was following out the old principle of tolerance which had become established in his mind during the preceding decade.

With the implication that art was superior to religion, Carlyle might not have been able to continue much longer his speculation on tolerance. But the end of the passage just quoted suggests that the grounds were shifting a little. And in the journal on November 12 the shift is clear. The issue was not strictly between art and religion. Instead it lay between the moral principle inculcated by modern art and the moral principle inculcated by an ancient religious creed. He thought that possibly the principle of tolerance manifested in art was the new moral principle for his own era.

[91] *Two Note Books*, p. 204.

This I begin to see, that Evil and Good are everywhere like Shadow and Substance: inseparable (for man); yet not hostile, only opposed. There is considerable significance in this fact—perhaps the *new* moral principle of our Era. (*How?*)—It was familiar to Goethe's mind.[92]—

In short, Carlyle was attempting to do the same sort of thing he had done before. Once he had re-defined reason and made it the dwelling place of religion. Now he was attempting to re-define religion to include tolerance instead of intolerance.

Five days later he made another important entry on the subject of tolerance. Incidentally, it tied up with the doctrine of unconsciousness, which he was then elaborating in his essay "Characteristics." The notebook entry ran as follows:

As it is but a small portion of our Thinking that we can articulate into Thoughts, so again it is but a small portion, properly only the outer surface of our morality that we can shape into Action, or into express Rules of Action. Remark farther that it is but the correct coherent shaping of this outer surface, or the incorrect incoherent monstrous shaping of it, and nowise the moral Force which shaped it, which lies under it, vague, indefinite, unseen, that constitutes what in common speech we call a moral conduct or an immoral. Hence too the necessity of tolerance, of insight, in judging of men. For the correctness of that same outer surface may be out of all proportion to the inward depth and quantity; nay often enough they are in inverse proportion; only in some highly favored individuals can the great endowment utter itself without irregularity. Thus in great men, with whom inward and as it were latent morality must ever be the root and beginning of greatness, how often do we find a conduct defaced by many a moral impropriety; and have to love them with sorrow! [93]

Carlyle realized, in fact he had long realized, the disproportion between the infinite nature of moral force and the finite nature of conventional moral standards. Instead of fixed standards of morality provided in the letter of the law, the new era demanded a differential that involved tolerance. It was to the recent German artists, rather than to the old-line religionists, that he looked for enlightenment upon this important new principle for society.

Naturally in the works that he wrote for immediate publication he stated his opinions with more caution than he used while jotting down his speculations in his private journal. But in the light of the journal entries concerning the principle of tolerance, the im-

[92] *Two Note Books*, p. 227.　　　[93] *Two Note Books*, pp. 228-229.

portance of tolerance as the new moral principle, and the implications of this principle in German literature, the following passages written also in 1831, for publication, take on special significance.

> In the nobler Literature of the Germans, say some, lie the rudiments of a new spiritual era, which it is for this and for succeeding generations to work out and realize.[94]

Literature seemed to him a branch of religion, and he believed that it always participated in the character of religion. But, he continued, " in our time, it [literature] is the only branch that still shows any greenness; and, as some think, must one day become the main stem." [95]   Change—change of all kinds—was on its way, but it would, he thought, obey the law of progress. And change would be for the better.

> . . . in all Poetry, Worship, Art, Society, as one form passes into another, nothing is lost: it is but the superficial, as it were the *body* only, that grows obsolete and dies; under the mortal body lies a *soul* which is immortal; which anew incarnates itelf in fairer revelation; and the Present is the living sum-total of the whole Past.
>
> In Change, therefore, there is nothing terrible, nothing supernatural: on the contrary, it lies in the very essence of our lot and life in this world. . . . Change, indeed, is painful; yet ever needful. . . . Nay, if we look well to it, what is all Derangement, and necessity of great Change, in itself such an evil, but the product simply of *increased resources* which the old *methods* can no longer administer; of new wealth which the old coffers will no longer contain?
>
> . . . Pyrrhonism and Materialism, themselves necessary phenomena in European Culture, have disappeared, and a Faith in Religion has again become possible and inevitable for the scientific mind. . . . [In] the higher Literature of Germany, there already lies, for him that can read it, the beginning of a new revelation of the Godlike; as yet unrecognised by the mass of the world; but waiting there for recognition, and sure to find it when the fit hour comes. This age also is not wholly without its Prophets.[96]

And the religious significance of literature joined with the social significance in the following long passage.

[94] *Essays*, II, 346.

[95] *Ibid.*, III, 23.

[96] *Ibid.*, III, 39-41. This whole idea of the permanent in the flux is also presented in *Sartor Resartus* under the figure of the Phoenix death-birth. And a statement that German literature contains a prophet and parts of a liturgy is also found in *Sartor Resartus*, p. 230.

It has been said, and may be repeated, that Literature is fast becoming all in all to us; our Church, our Senate, our whole Social Constitution. The true Pope of Christendom is not that feeble old man in Rome; nor is its Autocrat the Napoleon, the Nicholas, with his half-million even of obedient bayonets: such Autocrat is himself but a more cunningly-devised bayonet and military engine in the hands of a higher than he. The true Autocrat and Pope is that man, the real or seeming Wisest of the past age; crowned after death; who finds his Hierarchy of gifted Authors, his Clergy of assiduous Journalists; whose Decretals, written not on parchment, but on the living souls of men, it were an inversion of the laws of Nature to *dis*obey. In these times of ours, all Intellect has fused itself into Literature: Literature, Printed Thought, is the molten sea and wonder-bearing chaos, into which mind after mind casts forth its opinion, its feeling, to be molten into the general mass, and to work there; Interest after Interest is engulfed in it, or embarked on it: higher, higher it rises round all the Edifices of Existence; they must all be molten in it, and anew bodied forth from it, or stand unconsumed among its fiery surges. Woe to him whose Edifice is not built of true Asbest, and on the everlasting Rock; but on the false sand, and of the drift-wood of Accident, and the paper and parchment of antiquated Habit! For the power or powers, exist not on our Earth, that can say to that sea, Roll back, or bid its proud waves be still.

What form so omnipotent an element will assume; how long it will welter to and fro as a wild Democracy, a wild Anarchy; what Constitution and Organisation it will fashion for itself, and for what depends on it, in the depths of Time, is a subject for prophetic conjecture, wherein brightest hope is not unmingled with fearful apprehension and awe at the boundless unknown. The more cheering is this one thing which we do see and know: That its tendency is to be a universal European Commonweal; that the wisest in all nations will communicate and coöperate; whereby Europe will again have its true Sacred College, and Council of Amphictyons; wars will become rarer, less inhuman, and in the course of centuries such delirious ferocity in nations, as in individuals it already is, may be proscribed, and become obsolete for ever.[97]

Thus Carlyle in 1831 looked especially to German literature for the rudiments of a new spiritual era. He believed that in his time literature was the only branch of religion that showed vitality. And he considered it the greatest of social forces,—the smelting agency that would separate the true from the false in social institutions and would re-embody the true in new forms for the new era. The end of the long passage just quoted suggests a new harmony that literature might in the course of time bring between

[97] *Essays*, II, 369-370.

European nations.   Literature was rapidly assimilating the functions of religion.

Before the fusion between poetry and religion could actually take place, the principle of morals would need special consideration.   But Carlyle found the nature of morals very difficult to understand.   There were really two principles of morality in his mind.   The principle that he seemed to favor as the one fit for the new era stipulated a tolerant relationship, rather than the older hostile relationship, between the dualistic elements in man's life. This principle of tolerance he found inculcated in the writings of some of the German poets, most notably in the writings of Goethe. But however promising the principle that was sponsored by the Germans seemed, it was in conflict with the other principle, intolerance, which was sponsored by Carlyle's Puritan upbringing.   In its broadest terms the principle of tolerance, which he favored in 1831, was one of individualism.   It refused to judge all individuals alike by a fixed standard.   It would not consider an individual wrong to the quantitative extent that he deviated from the letter of a static law.   Instead of calculating morality by comparing the variable element of individual conduct with the fixed element of propriety, the principle of tolerance insisted that the true index of morality was the ratio between two variable elements, the individual's actual performance and his potentialities.   It demanded first that the orbit of the individual's genius, his potentialities, be known; then that the deviation of his actual performance from the orbit of his potentialities be measured; and finally that the ratio between the deviation and the orbit be computed as his moral aberration.   This principle of tolerance approved of the expansion of old fixed proprieties as soon as they became restrictive.   This expansive individualism shows continuity with the Old Testament prophetic tradition, with the New Testament Gospels, and with romanticism.   In short, tolerance provided for a positive morality. On the other hand, intolerance provided for a negative morality, a system of prescriptive conduct conforming to the law of external authority.   And this prescriptive or prohibitive conception of conduct shows continuity with the Old Testament legalistic tradition and with Puritanism.   Thus, it is only to be expected that the romantic-Puritan Carlyle would experience confusion as he attempted to understand morals and to choose the morality that would enter into his view of poetry and religion. And at the end of 1831, when he stated his hesitant belief in a moral system that embodied tolerance, he was doing more than indicating that the conflict in his mind was no longer one between poetry and religion. He was presenting the incongruous spectacle of a man with a Puritan upbringing trying to re-define religion so as to include a romantic expansive individualism. He was opening the door on the deepest struggle in him—the conflict between Puritanism and romanticism.

The results of this discussion concerning the relations between poetry and religion in Carlyle's mind up to 1832 may be stated briefly. For several years during his early manhood Carlyle considered reason an enemy to man's spiritual peace. But under the influence of German philosophy he acquired a favorable conception of reason and re-defined the province of this faculty. So complete was this change that, by 1829, reason seemed to him the unifier of religion and poetry. From one aspect of his faith in reason, Carlyle developed the principle of tolerance. This principle—that the true index of morality is the ratio between a man's performance and his potentialities—was well stated in the essay on Burns in 1828. And it became so much a part of his thought that it entered into his later judgments. Notwithstanding the fact that this principle was being developed at the same time that a conflict between religion and poetry was arising, the implication of this principle in the conflict was not apparent until a comparatively late date. Indeed, the conflict itself between religion and poetry had begun almost imperceptibly, with only a gradual shift in emphasis upon the elements. Early in his study of German literature Carlyle had come in contact with the notion that the beautiful is higher than the good. At first he had disapproved of this notion. But his further studies in Schiller, Goethe, and Fichte reinforced his growing estimate of the literary profession. In his mind, Fichte's learned men became literary men,—elect men, forming a perpetual priesthood and dispensing divine wisdom to their respective ages. Thus literature took on an increasing social and religious significance. And as Carlyle himself became more acutely aware of the need for social reform in his own time, he turned for guidance to literature rather than to the church. At length even the existing system of morals seemed doomed because of inadequacy. Meanwhile Carlyle pondered over the relative values of the good and the beautiful. Such men as Goethe and Schiller had considered goodness inferior to beauty. And Carlyle came to believe that this judgment was based upon a comparison of a hostile dualism with a harmonious dualism. Thus, for him the issue lay between intolerance and tolerance. When the issue was reduced to these terms in 1831, the old principle of tolerance that had been evolved during the preceding decade furnished the decision. By stating the problem in terms of intolerance and tolerance, Carlyle avoided a critical issue between religion and art, and instead proposed an issue between two systems of morals. The intolerant system, sponsored by his Puritan upbringing, was pitted against the tolerant system, sponsored by his German romantic sympathies. Thus, in ultimate terms, the struggle lay between Puritanism and romanticism. But the immediate aspect is more pertinent now. At the end of 1831, Carlyle's recognition that the conflict lay between two systems of morality, instead of between religion and poetry, left him with the notion that religion and poetry were to be united. And he believed that the common problem of both religion and poetry was to evolve and popularize a new tolerant morality. In short, a theoretical fusion had taken place between religion and poetry in Carlyle's mind.

CARLYLE'S VIEWS ON THE RELATION BETWEEN POETRY AND HISTORY UP TO EARLY 1832 [1]

During Carlyle's early twenties, his intellectual interests were numerous, and they changed rapidly. They included such subjects as natural theology, mathematics, astronomy, British philosophy, geology, miscellaneous works in various literatures, and law. It was while in the midst of this confusion of interests that he began reading the 18th century historians.[2] The effect was notable. For

[1] This article is the second of a series of three dealing with Carlyle's fusion of poetry, religion, and history by 1834. The first, "Carlyle's Views on the Relation between Poetry and Religion up to 1832," was published in *SP*, XXXIII (1936), pp. 57-92 (above, pp. 1-36). The third, and last, presents the actual fusion: "Carlyle's Fusion of Poetry, Religion, and History up to 1834" (below, pp. 57-85. None of these articles attempts to give a detailed exposition of Carlyle's indebtedness to German philosophy, his critical theory in literature, his religious tenets, his historical method, or his social doctrines. Separate studies of most of these elements in his intellectual development are already accessible to the reader. In addition to the ones mentioned in *SP*, XXXIII (1936), pp. 57-58 note (above, pp. 1-2), see C. F. Harrold's valuable article "Carlyle's General Method in *The French Revolution*," *PMLA*, XLIII (1928), 1150-1169, especially pp. 1150 and 1167-1168. This study is supplemented by part of Professor Harrold's recent book *Carlyle and German Thought* (New Haven, 1934), especially Chapter VI: "Carlyle and History," pp. 151-79. Also two of the standard biographies contain excellent comments on Carlyle as historian: J. A. Froude, *Thomas Carlyle . . . 1834-1881* (New York, 1884), I, 75-82; and J. Nichol, *Thomas Carlyle* (London, 1902), pp. 173-187 and 218. Carlyle's social doctrines are discussed in the following books: F. W. Roe, *The Social Philosophy of Carlyle and Ruskin* (London, 1921), especially pp. 88, 93, 95-96, 107, 112-119; Emery Neff, *Carlyle and Mill* (second ed., New York, 1926), especially Ch. V, pp. 208-221, on the influence of Saint-Simonism; Emery Neff, *Carlyle* (New York, 1932), especially Ch. IV: pp. 97-155; David Brooks Cofer, *Saint Simonism in the Radicalism of Thomas Carlyle* (College Station, Texas, 1931), especially p. 47; Louis Cazamian, *Carlyle*, Tr. by E. K. Brown (New York, 1932), especially Bk. II, Ch. III: "Social Philosophy," pp. 182-209.

[2] Thomas Carlyle, *Early Letters of Thomas Carlyle*, edited by C. E. Norton (London, 1886), I, 127 and 143-145. Thomas Carlyle, *Reminiscences*, edited by C. E. Norton (London, 1887), II, 28; David Masson, *Edinburgh Sketches and Memoirs* (London, 1892), pp. 263-264; William Allingham, *A Diary*, edited by H. Allingham and D. Radford (London, 1907), p. 232.

example, from the reading of Gibbon, he dated the final eradication
of his early orthodoxy.[3]   But years elapsed before the study and
writing of history became his primary interest.

During his late twenties, the more technical subjects in which
he had once been interested gave way in a marked degree to humane
subjects.   The biographical articles that he wrote for *The Edinburgh Encyclopedia* [4] and his preparations for writing a life of
Milton and for presenting historical sketches of the chief characters
who took part in the Civil Wars [5] indicate his growing interest in
human realities.   A slight examination of German literature had
opened to him a " new Heaven and new Earth." [6]   And further
study of the Germans resulted in a *Life of Schiller* [7] and a bio-

---

[3] Masson, *Edinburgh Sketches and Memoirs*, pp. 263-264.

[4] Between February, 1820 (see *Early Letters of Thomas Carlyle*, I,
276), and January, 1823 (see *The Love Letters of Thomas Carlyle and
Jane Welsh*, edited by A. Carlyle [New York, 1909], I, 146).   These
articles are to be found in the 5th volume of *Critical and Miscellaneous
Essays*, edited by H. D. Traill (London, 1899); in *Montaigne and Other
Essays Chiefly Biographical* (London, 1897); and in *The Edinburgh
Encyclopaedia*, edited by David Brewster (Edinburgh, 1830), Vol. XVI,
article " Pascal."   This article on Pascal, which is the best of the lot, has
not been reprinted.

[5] From March to May, 1822; see *Two Note Books of Thomas Carlyle*,
edited by C. E. Norton (New York, 1898), pp. 1-31, and *Early Letters of
Thomas Carlyle*, especially II, 56-57.

[6] A letter of August 4, 1820, in Moncure Daniel Conway, *Thomas
Carlyle* (New York, 1881), p. 184.

[7] The first version of this biography was written in three parts, between
April, 1823, and February, 1824.   And these parts were published serially
in *The London Magazine*.   Part I (finished in April, 1823: see *Love Letters*, I, 204) was published in *The London Magazine*, VIII, 381-400; Part
II (finished in November, 1823: see *Early Letters of Carlyle*, II, 245)
was published in *LM*, IX, 37-59; Part III (finished in February 1824:
see *Love Letters*, I, 332-334) was published in *LM*, X, 16-25, 149-163, 259-
269.   Then after the serial was complete, Carlyle revised the biography for
publication in book form.   His work on this final form was finished in
January, 1825 (see *Early Letters*, II, 305-306).   For the final text, see
The Life of Friedrich Schiller, edited by Traill (London, 1899).   Thus
the various stages in the development of this book serve as a valuable
index to the development of Carlyle's mind during nearly two years.   And
this index can be extended a little further back by taking into count the
note book entries that he made in preparation for Part I of the biography
(see the passages in *Two Note Books*, pp. 33-49, recorded in March, 1822).

graphical sketch of Goethe.[8]   These two works show a marked advance in the development of his interest in humane realism. And they also reveal a great advance in his favorable attitude toward aesthetics.[9]   Furthermore, his biographical and critical introductions to the authors included in *German Romance* [10] continue to show the realistic or historical tendency to some extent joined with aesthetic speculation: that is, they attempt to relate biographical developments and artistic processes.

But the fusion of history and poetry in Carlyle's mind was not as simple as those facts may seem to indicate.   Indeed, the process of fusion became seriously complicated.   The purpose of this paper is to examine these complications.   It will attempt to show how, at first, verisimilitude in poetry seemed sufficient; how his developing transcendentalism enabled him to see the ideal in the actual; how the abstract and the fictional lost caste in his mind; and how, finally, his deepened sense of the value of reality caused him to alter his early conception of poetry and to discard fiction.

In 1826 Carlyle looked upon poetic fiction as the purest truth.

The angels and demons that can lay prostrate our hearts in the nineteenth century must be of another and more cunning fashion than those that subdued us in the ninth.   To have attempted, to have begun this enterprise, may be accounted the greatest praise.   That Goethe ever meditated it, in the form here set forth, we have no direct evidence: but indeed such is the end and aim of high poetry at all times and seasons; for the fiction of the poet is not falsehood, but the purest truth; and if he would lead captive our whole being, not rest satisfied with a part of it, he must address us on interests that *are*, not that *were*, ours; and in a dialect which finds a response, and not a contradiction, within our bosoms.[11]

---

[8] The Introduction to *Meister's Apprenticeship* (see *Wilhelm Meister's Apprenticeship and Travels*, edited by Traill [London, 1907]); written in May, 1824 (see *Love Letters*, I, 363 and 371).

[9] Along with advances in these two respects, historical realism and aesthetics, these works show advance in the development of a favourable attitude toward reason and in the development of the principle of tolerance (see *SP*, XXXIII [1936], 63-71, or above, pp. 7-15).

[10] These introductions were written between April, 1825 (see *Love Letters*, II, 116-117 note), and August, 1826 (see *Love Letters*, II, 308). They are to be found in *German Romance*, edited by Traill (London, 1898), and in *Wilhelm Meister's Apprenticeship and Travels*. *The Travels*, with its introduction, first appeared in *German Romance*. *The Apprenticeship*, with its introduction, already alluded to in note 8, appeared in 1824.

[11] Introduction to *Wilhelm Meister's Apprenticeship and Travels*, ed. *cit.*, I, 29.

This endorsement of the fictions of the German master-poet was indeed enthusiastic. But the passage just quoted contains two minor pointers in the general direction of actuality rather than of fiction. The first of these is the stipulation that the poet must use contemporary interests instead of antiquated myths. The second is the suggestion that the poem should be fit for the reader's responsive acceptance rather than for his contradiction.

In October of the next year, 1827, he dealt with these same suggestions again. And this time the stress on reality was greater than before.

The poetry of Goethe . . . is no reminiscence, but something actually present and before us; no looking back into an antique Fairyland, divided by impassable abysses from the real world as it lies about us and within us; but a looking round upon that real world itself, now rendered holier to our eyes, and once more become a solemn temple, where the spirit of Beauty still dwells, and is still, under new emblems, to be worshipped as of old. . . . she [poetry] must dwell in Reality, and become manifest to men in the forms among which they live and move. And this is what we prize in Goethe, and more or less in Schiller and the rest. . . . The coldest sceptic, the most callous worldling, sees not the actual aspects of life more sharply than they are here delineated: the Nineteenth Century stands before us, in all its contradiction and perplexity; barren, mean, and baleful, as we have all known it; yet here no longer mean and barren, but enamelled into beauty in the poet's spirit. . . . [12]

In the same essay he touched upon Shakespeare's use of fiction.

Are these dramas of his not veri-similar only, but true; nay, truer than reality itself, since the essence of unmixed reality is bodied forth in them under more expressive symbols? [13]

Thus for Carlyle in 1827 such men as Goethe, Shakespeare, and Schiller might take the facts of life and add to them the consecration and the poet's dream. And this combination constituted truth. Verisimilitude, he still thought, could be truer than reality itself.

But Zacharias Werner was no such poet as Goethe, or Shakespeare, or Schiller. And by November 25, 1827, Carlyle thought Werner's fictional treatment of the Diet of Worms inferior in grandeur to the historical account.[14] He found great fault with

[12] *Critical and Miscellaneous Essays*, ed. cit., I, 65-66.
[13] *Ibid.*, I, 51.
[14] *Ibid.*, I, 125.

Werner's use of the supernatural and allegorical in the drama *Luther*.

> These half-allegorical, half-corporeal beings yield no contentment anywhere: Abstract Ideas, however they may put on fleshly garments, are a class of characters whom we cannot sympathize with or delight in. Besides, how can this mere embodiment of an allegory be supposed to act on the rugged materials of life, and elevate into ideal grandeur the doings of real men, that live and move amid the actual pressure of worldly things? [15]

The excellence that Carlyle found wanting in this kind of poetry was verisimilitude. And when he was writing about such poets as Werner, he felt free to condemn unreality of appearance. Not so, however, when he dealt with the great Goethe. This inconsistency is very noticeable when, in March, 1828, only a few months after the essay on Werner, Carlyle is discovered doing obeisance before the allegorical interlude *Helena* from Goethe's *Faust*.[16] He rationalized his attitude thus:

> . . . the grand point is to *have* a meaning, a genuine, deep and noble one; the proper form for embodying this, the form best suited to the subject and to the author, will gather round it almost of its own accord. We profess ourselves unfriendly to no mode of communicating Truth; which we rejoice to meet with in all shapes, from that of the child's Catechism to the deepest poetical Allegory. Nay, the Allegory itself may sometimes be the truest part of the matter.[17]

Wherever Goethe was concerned, Carlyle for many years yet was apt to temper his statements.[18]

But notwithstanding numerous exceptions, there is traceable in the records of the year 1828 a special interest in the use of the merely actual for purposes of poetry. The essay on Burns, which was finished by September 16, furnishes striking evidence. Clearness of vision, rather than perfection of utterance, seemed to Carlyle the characteristic of a poet.[19] For the poet, he said,

---

[15]*Ibid.*, I, 127-128.   [16] *Ibid.*, I, 146-197.   [17] *Ibid.*, I, 149.

[18] Indeed, in the same essay on *Helena*, he assumed an obligation to publish an English translation of Goethe's *Das Mährchen* (*Essays*, I, 196). But more than four years passed before he fulfilled the promise. Perhaps his most inexplicable infringment of judgment, even in favor of Goethe, was his effort at crystal gazing into this *Tale of Tales* as late as the summer of 1832 (*Ibid.*, II, 447-479).

[19] *Ibid.*, I, 272.

the Ideal world is not remote from the Actual, but under it and within it: nay, he is a poet, precisely because he can discern it there. . . . He is a *vates*, a seer; a gift of vision has been given him.[20]

Of course Carlyle was here discussing insight, not mere visual power. But out flew the terms and floated wide. And a few pages later he extended the poet's clearness of sight down to mere physical sight.[21] In this respect Burns seemed comparable with Homer.

In respect of mere clearness and minute fidelity, the *Farmer's* commendation of his *Auld Mare* . . . may vie with Homer's Smithy of the Cyclops, or yoking of Priam's Chariot.[22]

This was ultimate praise, in its way, for it seemed to Carlyle that Homer surpassed all other men in clearness of sight.[23] But he ranked the 18th century English novelists Richardson and Defoe at no great distance below the Greek poet in this particular.[24] Here, Carlyle was still concerning himself with verisimilitude. And no issue was yet drawn, or even distinction made, between fictional verisimilitude and historical actuality. Nevertheless the contributing shift of interest was in process. And little by little the thing appeared. For instance, during the fall of 1828 he was looking sharply at the actual world around him, seeing beyond it deep wonders.

Oh God, it is a fearful world, this we live in, a film spread over bottomless abysses, into which no eye has pierced.[25]

And on November 26th he said:

Is not this Thy world a mystery, and grand with Terror as well as Beauty! [26]

Before the year was out, he wrote De Quincy that he had the whole universe to study, for he understood less and less of it.[27]

---

[20] *Ibid.*, I, 272.
[21] *Ibid.*, I, 276.
[22] *Ibid.*, I, 276.
[23] *Ibid.*, I, 276-277.
[24] *Ibid.*, I, 276-277.
[25] J. A. Froude, *Thomas Carlyle* . . . 1795-1835 (New York, 1882), II, 40 n.
[26] *Letters of Thomas Carlyle*, 1826-1836, edited by C. E. Norton (London, 1889), p. 132.
[27] William Howie Wylie, *Thomas Carlyle, The Man and his Books* (third edition, London, 1881), p. 113.

As the new year, 1829, began, he was reading and studying for the second time "the most perfect of modern spirit-seers," Novalis.[28] Near the end of the essay that resulted from this study Carlyle quoted Tieck's statement on this German mystic:

For him it had become the most natural disposition to regard the commonest and nearest as a wonder, and the strange, the supernatural as something common. . . .[29]

This is precisely the natural supernaturalism that was growing up in Carlyle's own mind. It marks the influence of transcendentalism upon his changing view of reality. And his notebook entries show that he was aware of this change:

Has the mind its cycles and seasons like Nature, varying from the fermentation of *werden* to the clearness of *seyn*; and this again and again; so that the history of a man is like the history of the world he lives in? In my own case, I have traced two or three such vicissitudes: at present if I mistake not, there is some such thing at hand for me.[30]

Succeeding entries suggest that the change involved a new view of social actualities. Such actualities were assuming a new significance.

Above all things, I should like *to know England*, the essence of social life in this same little Island of ours. But how? . . . I have not even a *history* of the country, half precise enough.[31]

Shall we actually go and *ride* thro' England to see it?[32]

What is to become (next) of the world and the sciences thereof? Rather, what is to become of *thee* and thy science? Thou longest to *act* among thy fellow men, and canst (yet) scarcely *breathe* among them.[33]

Pray that your eyes be opened, that you may *see* what *is* before them! The whole world is built as it were, on Light and Glory; only that our *spiritual* eye must discern it. . . .[34]

In short, things that had heretofore attracted only his incidental attention were now becoming centers of observation.

Especially, social conditions were assuming the proportions of revelations. The social interest can be seen in the essay on Voltaire,

---

[28] *Two Note Books*, pp. 135 and 140, and *Letters of Thomas Carlyle*, p. 137.

[29] *Essays*, II, 53.

[30] *Two Note Books*, p. 132.

[31] *Ibid.*, p. 132.

[32] *Ibid.*, p. 134.

[33] *Ibid.*, p. 135.

[34] *Ibid.*, p. 136.

which was finished at the end of March, 1829.[35]   Carlyle looked upon the age of Voltaire as an experiment to decide the great question,

> With what degree of vigour a political system, grounded on pure Self-interest, never so enlightened, but without a God or any recognition of the godlike in man, can be expected to flourish. . . .[36]

And Scottish Carlyle turned to the example of German Luther as a corrective to the condition illustrated by Voltaire and France. He desired to write a life of the German reformer and to show him overturning and re-moulding society.   And he added:

> When are we to have another Luther?   Such men are needed from century to century: there seldom has been more need of one than now.[37]

In the essay " Signs of the Times " he looked at the society of his own era.   The mechanical and industrial revolution had increased the social maladjustments by widening the distance between rich and poor.[38]   He heard from all Europe the crying need for change, and felt the " deep-lying struggle in the whole fabric of society; a boundless grinding collision of the New with the Old." [39]   And he regarded the French Revolution as an offspring of this movement.[40] Furthermore, the notebook shows that he continued his examination of society after the completion of this essay.   To him, political economy seemed to have missed the heart of the matter.   Instead of giving " a scientific revelation of the whole secret mechanism whereby men cohere together in society," the political philosophers treated only such questions as money-making and exchange.[41]   They were materialists and utilitarians instead of mystical seers of natural supernaturalism.

Since political economy did not seem able to guide society, Carlyle looked to writers, the journalists, to develop this guidance. In " Signs of the Times " he said that the true Church of England lay in the editors of England's newspapers.[42]   This notion, at the same time that it imposed upon literature the guidance of human belief and conduct, implied a close connection between literature

---

[35] *Letters of Thomas Carlyle*, pp. 141 and 147.
[36] *Essays*, I, 462.
[37] *Two Note Books*, p. 140.
[38] *Essays*, II, 60.
[39] *Ibid.*, II, 82.
[40] *Ibid.*, II, 82.
[41] *Two Note Books*, pp. 143-145.
[42] *Essays*, II, 77.

and the actualities of human life.   Poetry itself, as that art is generally conceived, seemed to be giving way in Carlyle's esteem, to another form of composition.   By the end of October, he thought it partly true that no poet equalled his poem; but he thought it true, in a still deeper sense, that no poem equalled its poet.[43] Therefore he considered biography the species of composition that elucidated and completed the meanings of both poem and poet.[44] And he continued his statement on biography thus:

That ideal outline of himself, which a man unconsciously shadows forth in his writings, and which, rightly deciphered, will be truer than any other representation of him, it is the task of the Biographer to fill-up into an actual coherent figure, and bring home to our experience, or at least our clear undoubting admiration, thereby to instruct and edify us in many ways. Conducted on such principles, the Biography of great men, especially of great Poets, that is, of men in the highest degree noble-minded and wise, might become one of the most dignified and valuable species of composition.[45]

Thus Carlyle stressed the importance of humane fact, especially when it pertained to great men, when it was presented by the man of letters, and when it was interpreted properly.   This last matter, the edifying interpretation, was important.

The notion that the real is charged with the spiritual is a matter of interpretation.   And this notion of natural supernaturalism was growing rapidly in Carlyle's mind.   A notebook entry ran thus:

Wonderful Universe! Were our eyes but opened, what a 'secret' were it that we daily see and handle, without heed! [46]

And his attitude toward the use of actualities in poetry at the end of 1829 can be seen by an examination of his essay on Schiller.   In this essay he regarded Schiller's excellence as a simple one, lofty rather than expansive or varied; pure and ardent rather than great; partial rather than universal; reflective and philosophic rather than creative and poetic; systematic rather than intuitive.[47]

In fact it was toward the Ideal, not towards the Actual, that Schiller's faith and hope was directed.[48]

---

[43] *Ibid.*, II, 100.
[44] *Ibid.*, II, 100.
[45] *Ibid.*, II, 101.

[46] *Two Note Books*, p. 142.
[47] *Essays*, II, 197-198, 211.
[48] *Ibid.*, II, 193.

And he condemned Schiller's absorption in the abstract, at the cost of neglecting the common doings and interests of men.[49]

> . . . these latter, mean as they seem, are boundless in significance; for even the poorest aspect of Nature, especially of living Nature, is a type and manifestation of the invisible spirit that works in Nature. There is properly no object trivial or insignificant: but every finite thing, could we look well, is as a window, through which solemn vistas are opened into Infinitude itself.[50]

In the next paragraph he continued:

> Less in rising into lofty abstractions lies the difficulty, than in seeing well and lovingly the complexities of what is at hand. He is wise who can instruct us and assist us in the business of daily virtuous living; he who trains us to see old truth under Academic formularies may be wise or not, as it chances; but we love to see Wisdom in unpretending forms, to recognize her royal features under week-day vesture.[51]

Thereupon, he made his definition of humour, giving realism an important place in it.

> Humour is properly the exponent of low things; that which first renders them poetical to the mind. The man of Humour sees common life, even mean life, under the new light of sportfulness and love; whatever has existence has a charm for him. Humour has justly been regarded as the finest perfection of poetic genius. He who wants it, be his other gifts what they may, has only half a mind; an eye for what is above him, not for what is about him or below him. Now, among all writers of any real poetic genius, we cannot recollect one who, in this respect, exhibits such total deficiency as Schiller.[52]

What a falling off is here, in Carlyle's estimation of Schiller's poetry! But even while denouncing Schiller's practice, he valued Schiller's theories, and pointed with special approval to the *Aesthetic Letters*.[53]   At least Schiller understood what humour

---

[49] Strangely enough, in February 1824, Carlyle put Schiller ahead of all English writers in copying "lowly Nature." Burns showed that he could have equalled Schiller; no other Englishman had approached this equality. (*The London Magazine*, X, 260-262).

[50] *Essays*, II, 198-199. The similarity between the thought of this passage and that of the song of the Zeitgeist in *Faust* is unmistakable. And this flirtation with Pantheism is obvious also in *Sartor Resartus*, especially in Book III, Ch. VIII, "Natural Supernaturalism." However, Carlyle's strong moralistic bias prevented even Goethe's pantheism from retaining a permanent dominance over him.

[51] *Essays*, II, 199.   [52] *Ibid.*, II, 200-202.   [53] *Ibid.*, II, 191-192, 212.

was and showed his awareness of its essential worth.[54]   Carlyle's definition of humour was, along the one line, an adjustment to his own deepening sense of realism.

Temporarily during the next year, 1830, the possibility of a break between poetry and actuality became apparent. And this possibility, which appeared at the beginning of March, was fearfully attended. Carlyle was just stating his belief that he was about done with the Germans. He was just recording in his notebook his second notice that a change was coming over his mind ("some new and deeper view of the world is about to arise in me"). And he was again announcing that he had had mighty glimpses of natural supernaturalism (the actual and the ideal existing together). Then came the modest question.

What is Poetry? Do I really love Poetry? I sometimes fancy almost, not. The jingle of maudlin persons, with their mere (even genuine) 'sensibility' is unspeakably fatiguing to me. My greatly most delightful reading is, where some Goethe musically *teaches* me. Nay, *any* fact, relating especially to man, is still valuable and pleasing.[55]

In this comment upon his imagined distaste for poetry, sentimentality was the only element that Carlyle specifically mentioned as objectionable to him. But then he indicated three elements that contributed to his delight. The last of these was humane realism. It seems clear, then, that his imagined distaste for poetry was partly due to the fictional element usually contained in poetry.

At least the didactic and realistic tendencies observable in the passage just quoted from the notebook were consistent with his main activity during the year 1830. He was attempting to write a history of German literature. The introductory section of this book was separated from the rest in April [56] and was later published as an essay under the title "On History." At present, it need only be noted that, in an effort to blend poetry, religion, and history, he subordinated poetry to religion; and the outlook was made bright for a moralistic interpretation of history.[57] He stated the aim of the historian thus:

[He should aim] only at some picture of the things acted . . . [and] leave the inscrutable purport of them an acknowledged secret; or at most,

---

[54] *Ibid.*, II, 200-201.   [56] *Ibid.*, p. 154.
[55] *Two Note Books*, p. 151.   [57] *Essays*, II, 94.

in reverent Faith, . . . pause over the mysterious vestiges of Him, whose path is in the great deep of Time, whom History indeed reveals, but only all History, and in Eternity, will clearly reveal.[58]

This idea that human history is a developing revelation of the Divinity is what Carlyle called natural supernaturalism. And in one manifestation or another, it occurs more and more frequently in the notebook.

The idea that human history is a developing revelation of divinity implies a strong social interest as well as a strong religious interest. Both of these interests were again evident in a notebook entry written in August, 1830:

Is not the Christian Religion, is not every truly vital interest of mankind (?) a thing that *grows*? [59]

The progressive doctrines of Saint-Simon's social religion probably had some influence upon the entry just quoted, for the same page of the notebook contains the following entry.

Received about four weeks ago a strange letter from some *Saint-Simoniens* at Paris, grounded on my little *Signs of the Times*. These people have strange notions, not without a large spicing of truth, and are themselves among the *Signs*.[60]

Thereupon for the next few pages, Carlyle speculated upon social inequalities and political economy.[61] It was under these circumstances that the masterpiece *Sartor Resartus* was begun. One of the main significances of the complete book is its natural supernaturalism. That is, Diogenes Teufelsdröckh, the chief character in the book, attempted to look through the actualities of life (the clothes) and to see beyond them a spiritual reality which gave them significance. As early as September 7, the following anticipations of *Sartor Resartus* were recorded in the notebook. They unite Carlyle's social interests and his religious interests,—naturalism and supernaturalism.

I have strange glimpses of the power of spiritual Union, of Association among men of like object. Therein lies the true Element of Religion: it is a truly supernatural climate. . . . *Society* is a wonder of wonders; and Politics (in the right sense, far, very far from the common one) *is* the noblest Science.[62]

---

[58] *Ibid.*, II, 89.
[59] *Two Note Books*, p. 158.
[60] *Ibid.*, p. 158.

[61] *Ibid.*, pp. 158-60.
[62] *Ibid.*, pp. 164-165.

This notion that society is the wonder of wonders is a manifestation of the same natural supernaturalism that he had found in Novalis.

The Revolution of 1830 in France and the agitation for the passage of the Reform Bill in England joined with Saint-Simonian propaganda to increase Carlyle's interest in social affairs. A notebook entry of February, 1831, shows his diagnosis of social conditions.

All Europe is in a state of disturbance, of Revolution. About this very time they may be debating the question of British 'Reform,' in London. . . . The times are big with change. Will *one* century of constant fluctuation serve us, or shall we need two? Their Parl. Reforms, and all that, are of small moment; a beginning (of good & evil) nothing more. The whole frame of Society is rotten and must go for fuel-wood, and *where* is the new frame to come from? I know not, and no man knows.[63]

And he wrote further, in Teufelsdröckh's vein:

. . . Whiggism, I believe, is all but forever *done*. Away with Dilettantism and Machiavelism, tho' we should get Atheism and Sansculottism in their room! The latter are at least substantial things, and do not build on a continued *wilful* falsehood.[64]

Believing that centuries of change would be needed before a new adequate society would replace the old rotton one, he looked about him for the proper builders of the new. The radicals at least attempted to rid themselves of some of the old falsity.

While he was writing in this prophetic vein, he cast a glance at his own profession—Letters—and at its function. As he had already suggested in the essay "Signs of the Times," he still believed that literature was to take a leading part in the new society.

The only true Sovereigns of the world in these days are the Literary men (were there any such in Britain), the Prophets.[65]

But not only that. He considered literature the smelting agency that would separate the true social institutions from the false and would re-embody the true in new forms for the new era.[66] Along

---

[63] *Ibid.*, pp. 183-184.   [64] *Ibid.*, p. 186.
[65] *Ibid.*, p. 184. Similar notions are found in *Sartor Resartus*, edited by A. MacMechan (New York, 1905), pp. 39 and 229, and in *Essays* II, 369-370.
[66] *Essays*, II, 370.

with this high conception of literature and of the man of letters, Carlyle's conception of the poet was also rising. And instead of the break that had once seemed imminent between poetry and actuality in his mind, a reunion between them was rapidly taking place. But the identification of poetry and history involved the loss of fiction from poetry.

> What is a *Whole*? Or how, specially, *does* a Poem differ from Prose? . . .
>
> I see some vague outline of what a *Whole* is: also how an individual Delineation may be 'informed with the Infinite'; may appear hanging in the universe of Time & Space (partly): in which case is it a Poem and a Whole? Therefore, are the true Heroic Poems of these times to be written with the *ink of Science*? Were a correct philosophic Biography of a Man (meaning by philosophic *all* that the name can include) the only method of celebrating him? The true History (had we any such, or even generally any dream of such) the true Epic Poem?—I partly begin to surmise so.—What after all is the true proportion of St. Matthew to Homer, of the Crucifixion to the Fall of Troy! [67]

For the purpose of the present discussion, the leading thought in this passage from the notebook is the presumptive query that the epic poem of the new era should be written with the ink of science. That is, he suggested that the materials of the new poetry would be entirely credible actualities.

Believing men of letters the proper rulers and prophets of his age and considering literature the agency that would separate the true social institutions from the false and would re-embody the true in new forms for the new era, Carlyle labored through the spring and summer of 1831 to write *Sartor Resartus*. He meant this book for a reforming tract, as he himself said more than once.[68] But as usual, he believed that the only way to bring about a lasting reform of the utterly worn out society was to bring about moral reformation of the individuals in it.[69] Thus the first step of the great social reformation to which Teufelsdröckh looked forward was for man to escape from the besetting sins of materialism, mechanization, and utilitarianism, into a spiritual interpretation

---

[67] *Two Note Books*, pp. 187-188.

[68] J. W. Goethe and Thomas Carlyle, *Correspondence between Goethe and Carlyle*, edited by C. E. Norton (London, 1887), pp. 290-291. J. A. Froude, *Thomas Carlyle . . . 1795-1835* (New York, 1882), II, 145.

[69] *Essays*, II, 82; III, 160-161; and *Two Note Books*, pp. 205-206, 274.

of the actualities of life.   *Sartor Resartus* was an introduction to
the actual as the realm of wonder.

Art thou a grown baby, then, to fancy that the Miracle lies in miles of
distance, or in pounds avoirdupois of weight; and not to see that the true
inexplicable God-revealing Miracle lies in this, that I can stretch forth my
hand at all; that I have free Force to clutch aught therewith? [70]

Nor did man need philosophic systems wherewith to understand
the wonderful actualities about him and in him.   Philosophy could
not answer the sphinx riddle of man's life.

Pity that all Metaphysics had hitherto proved so inexpressibly unproduc-
tive! . . . What are your Axioms, and Categories, and Systems, and
Aphorisms? Words, words.[71]

. . . all Speculation is by nature endless, formless, a vortex amid vor-
tices. . . . [72]

This attitude toward metaphysical speculation reached its culmination in " Characteristics."   Both his feeling of the futility of
metaphysical speculation and his animosity against utilitarian self-
consciousness manifested themselves again in his text for this
essay: " the sign of health is Unconsciousness." [73]   In his introduction he wrote, " The beginning of Inquiry is Disease. . . . " [74]
Further, he repeated:

Nay, already, as above hinted, the mere existence and necessity of a
Philosophy is an evil.
. . . what Theorem of the Infinite can the Finite render complete? [75]

Thus, in 1831, in his tracts for the times, he insisted that men's
greatest possibilty lay in seeing the infinite significance of their
own limited existences and in realizing the moral regeneration
that comes from faithfully pursuing their own lines of duty, instead
of spending their time in theorizing on political and philosophic
systems.   He publicly denounced speculation on systematic philos-

---

[70] *Sartor Resartus, ed. cit.*, p. 238.   [73] *Essays*, III, 4.
[71] *Ibid.*, p. 47.   [74] *Ibid.*, III, 2.
[72] *Ibid.*, p. 177.
[75] *Ibid.*, III, 25.   See also III, 26-27.   On August 28, 1841, Carlyle wrote:
" It is many years since I ceased reading German or any other metaphysics, and gradually came to discern that I had happily got done with
that matter altogether."   Francis Espinasse, *Literary Recollections and
Sketches* (London, 1893), p. 58.

ophy,—a thing which for several years he had more and more renounced in private.

It was to the actualities of life, good and bad, that Carlyle turned. Even in the confusion and ignorance of the streets of London he tried to see a revelation of spirit.

" . . . *God is in it*: here, even here, is the Revelation of the Infinite in the Finite; a majestic Poem (tragic, comic or epic), couldst thou but read it and recite it! Watch it then; study it, catch the secret of it, and proclaim the same in such accent as is given thee.[76]

The whole world, it seemed to him, was growing more and more of a supernatural revelation, infinitely stern, infinitely grand; and he wondered if he would ever succeed " in *copying* a little therefrom." [77]   Thus his interest in society grew, and he insisted that the actualities of human life should be seen upon a spiritual background and should be considered a supernatural revelation. And as this notion developed, he regarded these actualities of human life as the proper material for poetry.

One more impressive piece of evidence will suffice to establish Carlyle's principle of realism at the beginning of 1832. It is taken from the essay on Boswell's *Life of Johnson*, which was the chief work that Carlyle wrote during his first winter in London. Because of length, the essay was published in two parts: " Biography," and " Boswell's Life of Johnson." The first part, " Biography," is of primary importance here because it goes further than Carlyle had gone before in his stress on actualities as the materials of poetry. Using the fictional character Professor Gottfried Sauerteig as his mouthpiece, Carlyle plainly denounced fiction.

The significance, even for poetic purpose, . . . that lies in REALITY is too apt to escape us; is perhaps only now beginning to be discerned.

Fiction, while the feigner of it knows that he is feigning, partakes, more than we suspect, of the nature of *lying* . . . [78]

This is strong language. Possibly there was an element of Puritanism lurking in the composition of this hypothetical Professor. The unvarnished meaning of the utterance against fiction

[76] *Two Note Books*, p. 211: October 22-24, 1831.
[77] *Ibid.*, p. 238: January, 1832.
[78] *Essays*, III, 49.

is remarkably similar to the notions of the Scottish Presbyterian James Carlyle, for whose death his son Thomas had mourned less than two months at the time of that writing. Carlyle Senior had long forbidden the reading of any fiction in his house.[79] He had objected especially to *The Arabian Nights' Tales* as "those down-right lies."[80]

But the fictitious German Professor had read and thought widely, and he could justify his statement more eloquently than could the Scottish Peasant. It was thus that Professor Sauerteig explained his own viewpoint:

All Mythologies were once Philosophies; were *believed*: the Epic Poems of old time . . . were Histories, and understood to be narratives of *facts*.[81]

In so far as Homer's gods were employed as mere ornamental fringes, just so far, Sauerteig thought, was Homer a hollow, false singer, pleasing only a portion of man's mind.[82]

Imagination is, after all, but a poor matter when it has to part company with Understanding, and even front it hostilely in flat contradiction. . . . Belief is, indeed, the beginning and first condition of all spiritual Force whatsoever: only in so far as Imagination, were it but momentarily, is *believed*, can there be any use or meaning in it, any enjoyment of it.[83]

As an illustration of his meaning, Sauerteig pointed to the use of the supernatural in epic poetry.

. . . the instant it has ceased to be authentically supernatural, and become what you call 'Machinery': sweep it out of sight (*schaff' es mir vom Halse*)![84]

Superannuated lumber—at best, cast raiment—were his terms for what he called "the dead Pagan gods of an *Epigoniad* . . . , the dead-living Pagan-Christian gods of a *Lusiad*, the concrete-abstract, evangelical-metaphysical gods of a *Paradise Lost*."[85] And he thought that the farther one receded from the entire credibility of the primitive performances in epic poetry, when poetry was true poetry and inspired, the more impossible it became to produce other than a pretense of poetry.[86]

---

[79] M. D. Conway, *Thomas Carlyle*, (N. Y., 1881), p. 27. Carlyle, *Reminiscences, ed. cit.*, I, 14.

[80] Conway, *op. cit.*, p. 27. Charles E. Norton, *Letters of Charles Eliot Norton* (Boston, 1913), I, 438. Carlyle, *Reminiscences*, I, 29.

[81] *Essays*, III, 49-50.

[82] *Ibid.*, III, 49-50.

[83] *Ibid.*, III, 50.

[84] *Ibid.*, III, 50.

[85] *Ibid.*, III, 51.

[86] *Ibid.*, III, 51.

Even if the *probable* were substituted for the *impossible* in fiction, Sauerteig thought that the evil would be much mended but by no means completely cured.[87]   The result would be an only partially living modern novel.[88]   But this novel could, sometimes, be given momentary credence.[89]

Thus, here and there, a *Tom Jones*, a *Meister*, a *Crusoe*, will yield no little solacement to the minds of men; though still immeasurably less than a *Reality* would, were the significance thereof as impressively unfolded, were the genius that could so unfold it once given us by the kind Heavens. Neither say thou that proper Realities are wanting: for Man's Life, now, as of old, is the genuine work of God; wherever there is a Man, a God also is revealed, and all that is Godlike: a whole epitome of the Infinite, with its meanings, lies enfolded in the Life of every Man. Only, alas, that the Seer to discern this same Godlike, and with fit utterance *un*fold it to us, is wanting, and may long be wanting! [90]

But Sauerteig was hopeful. He believed that man had lost none of his spiritual endowments.[91]   Even the highest of these endowments still remained,—the power of revealing poetic beauty and of adequately receiving it.[92]

Not the material, not the susceptibility is wanting; only the Poet, or long series of Poets, to work on these. True, alas too true, the Poet *is* still utterly wanting, or all but utterly: nevertheless have we not centuries enough before us to produce him in? Him and much else!—I, for the present, will but predict that chiefly by working more and more on REALITY, and evolving more and more wisely *its* inexhaustible meanings; and, in brief, speaking forth in fit utterance whatsoever our whole soul *believes*, and ceasing to speak forth what thing soever our whole soul does not believe,—will this high emprise be accomplished, or approximated to.[93]

These were the anti-fictional sayings of Sauerteig.

And in this same essay, " Biography," Carlyle in his proper person made a statement to the same effect concerning fiction and reality.

Great truly is Invention; nevertheless, that is but a poor exercise of it with which Belief is not concerned. . . . Nay, perhaps, if we consider well, the highest exercise of Invention has, in very deed, nothing to do with Fiction; but is an invention of new Truth, what we can call a Revelation; which last does undoubtedly transcend all other poetic efforts. . . .[94]

---

[87] *Ibid.*, III, 50-51.

[88] *Ibid.*, III, 52.

[89] *Ibid.*, III, 51-52.

[90] *Ibid.*, III, 52.

[91] *Ibid.*, III, 53.

[92] *Ibid.*, III, 53.

[93] *Ibid.*, III, 53.

[94] *Ibid.*, III, 53-54.

He believed that the struggle of human freewill against material necessity, which every man's life more or less victoriously exhibits,

is that which above all else, or rather inclusive of all else, calls the Sympathy of mortal hearts into action; and whether as acted, or as represented and written of, not only is Poetry, but is the sole Poetry possible.[95]

This was Carlyle's principle of poetic realism, enunciated in March, 1832. In it true human history and true poetry were considered one.

The gradual development of Carlyle's theoretical fusion of history and poetry can be restated without the details. Between 1820 and 1825 his earlier technical studies gave way in great measure to humane studies. And he became known as a biographer of German writers and a translator and critic of German literature. In 1826, at the same time that he considered poetic fiction the highest human truth, he demanded that the poet substitute contemporary interests for antiquated myths, and that the poem be fit to enlist the reader's responsive acceptance rather than his contradiction. Poetry " must dwell in Reality, and become manifest to men in the forms among which they live and move." For a while he was content with verisimilitude. Or, in the case of Goethe, he was content with an allegorical presentation of truth. But as his transcendental notion of " natural supernaturalism " developed, he more and more regarded actualities as revelations of the ideal or the supernatural. Society seemed to him the wonder of wonders. The history of man became to him a developing revelation of Divinity. He turned from fiction to fact. In 1829 he condemned Schiller's absorption in abstractions to the neglect of the common doings and interests of men. He defined humour as the exponent of low things, and regarded it as the finest perfection of poetic genius. In 1830, prompted to some extent by his growing love of actualities and by his growing distrust of fiction, he suspected that he did not really love poetry. But as his social interest developed, he could find no more appropriate guide for society during its much needed social reform than the genuine man of letters. And, being a man of letters himself, he wrote *Sartor Resartus* as a reforming tract, first for individuals and then,

[95] *Ibid.*, III, 45.

through them, for society. While this interest in society had grown, his interest in systematic philosophy had diminished. And in *Sartor* and in " Charactistics " he denounced systematic philosophy as futile. Meanwhile, on the other hand, as his interest in society developed, an alliance grew up in his mind between society and literature. And, instead of drifting away from poetry, as he had once feared doing, he merely altered his definition of poetry. By early 1832 this change in his conception of poetry was clearly enunciated. He believed that the highest exercise of poetic invention had " in very deed, nothing to do with Fiction." The struggle of man's free will against material necessity " not only is Poetry, but is the sole Poetry possible." Thus Carlyle's principle of poetic realism, stated in March, 1832, insisted that history and poetry are one.

CARLYLE'S FUSION OF POETRY, HISTORY,
AND RELIGION BY 1834 [1]

As the result of several converging lines of development, Carlyle in 1831 considered literature the highest activity of man. During less than a decade he had made some new definitions. He had re-defined reason to accommodate his conception of the German *Vernunft* and to reconcile a conflict between head and heart.[2] In the domain of reason both poetry and religion seemed to abide. He had also re-defined poetry.[3]   According to his new conception, poetry should turn from fiction to fact as the source of its materials. It should assimilate from history the function of presenting in credible form the actual conditions of human life. Furthermore, he was looking forward to a changed moral system, in preparation for the new era. He believed that literature, by presenting good and evil tolerantly, would furnish the moral principle that was fit for the new era.[4] That is, to Carlyle's mind, poetry would assimilate from religion the function of interpreting the relation between the dualistic elements of good and evil which provided the needed conflict in the drama of life. From 1832 until he began his permanent London residence in 1834, he attempted to elaborate into greater clearness the glimpses that he had caught by late 1831

---

[1] This paper is the third, and last, of a series of articles dealing with Carlyle's fusion of poetry, history, and religion. The first of the series is " Carlyle's Views on the Relation between Religion and Poetry up to 1832." *Studies in Philology*, XXXIII (1936), 57-92 (above, pp. 1-36). The second article is " Carlyle's Views on the Relation between Poetry and History up to early 1832." *SP*, XXXIII (1936), 487-506 (above, pp. 37-56). For some special discussions of Carlyle's philosophic, religious, social, and critical tenets, see the bibliographical notes at the beginnings of the first two articles. (Since this paper was accepted for publication, Professor C. F. Harrold's " The Nature of Carlyle's Calvinism " has appeared in *SP*, XXXIII (1936), 475-486.)

[2] For a discussion of this point see " Carlyle's Views on the Relation between Religion and Poetry up to 1832," *SP*, XXXIII, 58-69 (above, pp. 2-13).

[3] For a discussion see " Carlyle's Views on the Relation between Poetry and History up to early 1832," *SP*, XXXIII (1936), 487-506 (above, pp. 37-56).

[4] For a discussion see " Carlyle's views on the Relation between Religion and Poetry up to 1832," *SP*, XXXIII, 73-92 (above, pp. 17-36).

of a possible fusion of poetry with history and religion. The present discussion will trace the details of that elaboration as it took place.

Probably literature has seldom carried more social responsibility than it did in Carlyle's mind at the end of 1831. He thought that the new birth of society depended upon the slow development of character and insight in individuals.[5] And, looking to literature rather than to any church or any political party to bring about this development, he wondered what his own next literary duty should be. On October 10, 1831, this question took form as an entry in the journal.

> . . . *what* were the true duty of a man; were it to stand utterly aloof from Politics (not ephemeral only, for that of course, but generally from all speculation about social systems &c. &c.) ; or is not perhaps the very want of this time, an infinite want of Governors, of Knowledge how to govern itself?—Canst *thou* in any measure spread abroad Reverence over the hearts of men? That were a far higher task than *any* other. Is it to be done by Art; or are men's minds as yet shut to Art, and open only at best to oratory; not fit for a *Meister*, but only for a better and better *Teufelsdreck; Denk' und schweig!* [6]

But since publishers declined Teufelsdröckh's *Sartor Resartus,* a course of lectures began to seem more feasible than a work of art.

> . . . London is fit for no higher *Art* than that of Oratory: they understand nothing of Art; scarcely one of them anything at all.[7]

Thus the important year 1831 ended, with Carlyle in London, speculating on the kind of art that he could produce suitable to guide his fellow men in the new era.

In 1832 Carlyle was using old terms with new meanings. The essay on Biography, which was finished in March, 1832, contained a discussion of the prospects for poetry in the new era. There emerged from that discussion the suggestion that the poet should use the historical material of man's actual life, and that he should give the material a religious interpretation,—should see in it a revelation of Divinity. The struggle between human free-will and material necessity, said Carlyle, " not only is Poetry, but is the sole Poetry possible." [8] And Carlyle's mouthpiece, Sauerteig, added:

[5] Thomas Carlyle, *Critical and Miscellaneous Essays* (London, 1899), II, 82, and III, 160-161. See also *Two Note Books of Thomas Carlyle,* edited by C. E. Norton (New York, 1898), pp. 205-206, 274.

[6] *Two Note Books,* pp. 203-204.

[7] *Ibid.,* p. 212.   [8] *Essays,* III, 45.

. . . Man's Life, now, as of old, is the genuine work of God; wherever there is a Man, a God also is revealed, and all that is Godlike: a whole epitome of the Infinite, with its meanings, lies enfolded in the Life of every Man.[9]

For years Carlyle had insisted on the spiritual significance of all human actualities. Now human actualities seemed to him the only materials for poetry. A month later he wrote in his notebook that the deepest problem of his time was the adjustment between pulpit and press, that is, the adjustment between the old church and the new.

The grand Pulpit is now the Press; the true Church (as I have said twenty times of late) is the Guild of Authors. How these *two* Churches and Pulpits (the velvet-cushion one and the metal-type one) are to adjust their mutual relations and cognate workings: this is a problem which some centuries may be taken up in solving. It is the deepest thing to be solved in these days.[10]

From what has gone before, it is obvious that, in Carlyle's mind, there would be at least two major considerations in the adjustment between the old and the new agencies for presenting religious truth. One consideration would be the use of actual credible facts, good and bad, from human life. Another would be the tolerant portrayal of these dualistic elements. Presumably these two considerations would weight the scales in favor of the " metal-type " pulpit—literature.

Speculating on the functions of literature in the new era, and in particular, it would seem, on the moral principle that literature was to teach to society, Carlyle turned again to Goethe:

he still shines with his direct radiance; his inspired words are to abide in living hearts, as the life and inspiration of thinkers, born and still unborn. Some fifty years hence, his thinking will be found translated, and ground down, even to the capacity of the diurnal press; acts of parliament will be passed in virtue of him:—this man, if we consider of it, is appointed to be ruler of the world.[11]

The death of the great German in March, 1832, drew from Carlyle an eloquent funeral oration:

Goethe, it is commonly said, made a New Era in Literature; a Poetic Era began with him, the end or ulterior tendencies of which are yet nowise

---

[9] *Ibid.*, III, 52.
[10] *Two Note Books*, pp. 263-264.   [11] *Essays*, II, 373: by March, 1832.

generally visible. This common saying is a true one; and true with a far deeper meaning than, to the most, it conveys. . . . The true Sovereign of the world, who moulds the world like soft wax, . . . is he who lovingly *sees* into the world; the " inspired Thinker," whom in these days we name Poet. The true Sovereign is the Wise Man.[12]

Carlyle admitted that the impulse of a great man on world movements was slow. But in spite of the fact that it might require one or two generations to proclaim itself and become palpable to all men, and one or two more to reach its acme,[13] he believed that the authentic impulse for the society of the new era was to be found in Goethe's writings:

A poor reader . . . were he who discerned not here the authentic rudiments of that same New Era, whereof we have so often had false warning. Wondrously, the wrecks and pulverised rubbish of ancient things, institutions, religions, forgotten noblenesses, made alive again by the breath of Genius, lie here in new coherence and incipient union, the spirit of Art working creative through the mass; that *chaos*, into which the eighteenth century with its wild war of hypocrites and sceptics had reduced the Past, begins here to be once more a *world*.—This, the highest that can be said of written Books, is to be said of these: there is in them a New Time, the prophecy and beginning of a New Time. The corner-stone of a new social edifice for mankind is laid there; firmly, as before, on the natural rock: far-extending traces of a ground-plan we can also see; which future centuries may go on to enlarge, to amend and work into reality. These sayings seem strange to some; nevertheless they are not empty exaggerations, but expressions, in their way, of a belief, which is not now of yesterday; perhaps when Goethe has been read and meditated for another generation, they will not seem so strange.[14]

Just what Carlyle meant by " The corner-stone of a new social edifice for mankind " and by the " far-extending traces of a ground-plan " he does not here make clear.[15] It is possible that the ground-plan of the new social edifice had something to do with the harmo-

---

[12] *Ibid.*, II, 376-377: by April 26, 1832.

[13] *Ibid.*, II, 378.   [14] *Ibid.*, II, 381.

[15] In *Sartor Resartus*, which was finished by August 4, 1831, Teufelsdröckh had alluded to the universality of hero-worship as the corner-stone of all politics: " In which fact, that Hero-worship exists, has existed, and will forever exist, universally among Mankind, mayest thou discern the corner-stone of living-rock, whereon all Polities for the remotest time may stand secure." (*Sartor Resartus*, edited by A. MacMechan [revised edition, Boston, 1905], p. 228). At least the language of the passage from *Sartor* is much the same as the language in the later *Leichenrede* on Goethe, quoted above.

nious system of morality which he had found suggested in Goethe's writings. And he may have considered the principle of tolerance, with which he had long been concerned, the corner-stone upon which the edifice was to be erected. It is certain that he had for some time speculated upon the principle of tolerance as the new moral principle. Furthermore, in a long essay on Goethe's *Works,* finished in July, he pointed to Goethe's " perfect tolerance for all men and all things." [16] And he indicated the principle of tolerance in his summary of Goethe's notable contributions to modern times.

The question, Can man still live in devoutness, yet without blindness or contraction; in unconquerable steadfastness for the right, yet without tumultuous exasperation against the wrong; as an antique worthy, yet with the expansion and increased endowment of a modern? is no longer a question, but has become a certainty, an ocularly-visible fact.[17]

Finally, it was in August, 1832, that Carlyle wrote his introductory comments on Goethe's *Das Mährchen.* Teufelsdröckh was again his spokesman. He considered that fantastic tale a wonderful emblem of universal history and of this age of transition, the deepest poem of its kind in existence, the only true prophecy emitted for centuries.[18] After writing that commentary, Carlyle turned his attention to other matters. But his faith in Goethe's guidance was not yet exhausted. And he was probably not yet aware that, except for subsequent lectures, he had closed his career as an interpreter of German literature.

During the spring and summer of 1832, while he was still confused in his speculation on morals, his interests were gradually turning toward the history of the French Revolution and apparently also toward a creative literary work. The story of the archquack, Cagliostro, which had caught the interest of Schiller and Goethe, had attracted him.[19] But Carlyle's own study of events connected with revolutionary France had not yet progressed far enough to furnish materials for a narrative. And his earlier attempts at narrative had, he felt, fallen short of artistic excellence. A notebook entry of July 22 furnishes a clue to his intellectual condition at the time.

[16] *Essays*, II, 438.   [17] *Ibid.*, II, 440.   [18] *Ibid.*, II, 449, 479, note 2.
[19] Macvey Napier, *Selections from the Correspondence of Macvey Napier, Esq.*, edited by his son (London, 1879), p. 125.

> As yet I have never risen into the region of creation. Am I approaching
> it? *Ach Gott! sich nähern dem unaussprechlichen.*[20]

That is, in spite of all shortcomings, he apparently believed that
he was drawing nearer to the realm of art. But, unfortunately for
his peace of mind, he lacked some of the most essential elements
that enter into a creative work. Even the subject that he was
eventually to treat, the French Revolution, was not yet determined
in his mind. His specific knowledge of the material concerning
any phase of it was inadequate. His poetic technique in the writing
of history was untried. And his moral interpretation of the phenomena of human history was unresolved. Before his next creative
work could be written, each of these elements in it had to be
matured, and all of them brought together. By an organic development along lines that have already been pointed out, these
elements were actually matured and united within the next two
years. But in 1832, Carlyle was still groping his way toward that
fusion of history, poetry, and religion.

Possibly the main obstacle to that actual fusion can be seen in
a notebook entry of August 8, concerning morals.

> I cannot understand *Morals*. Our current Moral Law (even that of
> philosophers) affronts me with all manner of perplexities. *Punishment*
> neither is nor can be in proportion to fault; for the commonest of all
> examples take the case of an erring woman.
> . . . Where are the limits of conscience and honor? what relation (even
> for the anti-gigman) do the two mutually bear? Moral *force* and moral
> *correctness*—how shall the litigation be settled between these? Ought
> there to *be* any unpardonable offense? Ought the judge in any case to say
> irrevocably, *Be thou outcast* (as proud fathers have done to erring
> daughters for instance)? The world has declared, Yes. Neither is there
> wanting some ground for it. Necessity rules our existence: Man should
> step in and be as stern as Necessity, and *take the word out of its mouth.*
> Perhaps; yet not with clear certainty. This is ' the Place of Hope.' Should
> man's mind have sudden boundless transitions of that sort; have *vaporific
> points*, and *freezing points*, or should it not? *Weiss nicht.* It is all con-
> fused to me: seems to be all refounding itself. Happily the practical is
> no wise dubious.[21]

For the present, he decided on intolerance.

> Toleration . . . is miserably mistaken; means for most part only in-
> difference and contempt: *Verachtung, ja Nichtachtung.* What is bad *is*

---

[20] J. A. Froude, *Thomas Carlyle . . . 1795-1835* (New York, 1897),
II, 229.

[21] *Ibid.*, II, 247-248.

a thing to be the sooner the better *abolished*. Whether this imply *hatred* or not will depend on circumstances. Not toleration, therefore, but the quickest possible abolition: that were our rule. A wicked hatred, in abolishing, *substitutes* new badness (as bad or worse). The pure, *praiseworthy,* useful Hatred were that which abolished and did not substitute.[22]

And on August 11, he continued his justification of intolerance.

. . . evil must always continue: yet not this evil and that evil. *The* thing convicted of falsehood *must* be forthwith cast out: the Radical is a believer, of the gross, heathen sort; yet our only believer in these times.[23]

Although in August, 1832, Carlyle defended intolerance by calling it "The pure, *praiseworthy,* useful Hatred," his decision on the principles of morals was not settled.

In the essay "Diderot," which was finished by October 15, 1832, he took up a position diametrically opposed to the bleak position that he had occupied when he wrote the passages in his private journal concerning the old issue between tolerance and intolerance. That divergence shows his indecision. In "Diderot" he continued his habitual practice of regarding self-denial as the beginning of all moral action. And he admitted a connection between it and the ascetic system of morals. But he argued against the return of asceticism to dominance. He believed that it was possible to discern the filaments of a nobler system, wherein self-denial would be included as one harmonious element.[24] Though his statement in the essay was honestly uncertain and consequently vague, the general tenor of it is unmistakable.

Who knows, for example, what new unfoldings and complex adjustments await us, before the true relation of moral Greatness to moral Correctness, and their proportional value, can be established? How, again, is perfect tolerance for the Wrong to coexist with an ever-present conviction that Right stands related to it, as a God does to a Devil,—an Infinite to an opposite Infinite? How, in a word, through what tumultuous vicissitudes, after how many false partial efforts, deepening the confusion, shall it at length be made manifest, and kept continually manifest, to the hearts of men, that the Good is not properly the highest, but the Beautiful; that the true Beautiful (differing from the false, as Heaven does from Vauxhall) comprehends in it the Good?[25]

Thus as Carlyle pushed further, through a study of Diderot and his times, his own inquiry into the circumstances of the French

[22] *Ibid.*, II, 248.
[23] *Ibid.*, II, 249.
[24] *Essays*, III, 239.
[25] *Ibid.*, III, 239-240.

Revolution, he gave his clearest enunciation of what he considered the new moral principle of the new era. That passage was a plea for the tolerant relationship between the dualistic elements in human life. But his confusion was not cleared. For over a year, as will be shown, he vacillated between the two moral principles before he dismissed such speculation on virtue as futile.

Meanwhile, despite his confusion over morals, his purpose to fuse history, poetry, and religion continued. Though the element of realism did not cause him as much trouble as the element of morality, it was equally a part of the desired fusion. And in Diderot's writings he found some valuable contributions concerning artistic realism.

> . . . Diderot stands forth as the main originator, almost the sole one in his own country, of that many-sided struggle towards what is called Nature, and copying of Nature, and faithfulness to Nature: a deep indispensable truth, subversive of the old error; yet under that figure, only a half-truth, for Art too is Art, as surely as Nature is Nature; which struggle, meanwhile, either as half-truth or working itself into a whole truth, may be seen, in countries that have any Art, still forming the tendency of all artistic endeavour.[26]

The crux of the passage may be restated thus. Diderot's principle of realism comprised only a half-truth, in that it fell short of natural supernaturalism by lacking the second member. That is, Diderot's naturalism was not suffused with supernaturalism; he did not see that the highest significance of matter was spirit. The spiritual significance of the universe was of course an old doctrine to the author of *Sartor Resartus*.

Elsewhere in the essay on Diderot Carlyle revealed something of his own theory of realism in poetry, which is one aspect of the three-fold fusion. Carlyle's statement turns on actuality and credibility in the literature of the new era.

> Day after day looking at the high destinies which yet await Literature, which Literature will ere long address herself with more decisiveness than ever to fulfil, it grows clearer to us that the proper task of Literature lies in the domain of BELIEF; within which "Poetic Fiction," as it is charitably named, will have to take a quite new figure, if allowed a settlement there. Whereby were it not reasonable to prophesy that this exceeding great multitude of Novel-writers and suchlike, must, in a new generation, gradually do one of two things: either retire into nurseries, and work for children, minors and semifatuous persons of both sexes;

---

[26] *Ibid.*, III, 244.

or else, what were far better, sweep their Novel-fabric into the dust-cart, and betake them with such faculty as they have to understand and record what is *true*,—of which, surely, there is, and will forever be, a whole Infinitude unknown to us, of infinite importance to us! Poetry, it will more and more come to be understood, is nothing but higher Knowledge; and the only genuine Romance (for grown persons) Reality.[27]

Again and again he insisted that the actualities of human life were the proper materials for poetry.

Following out the conception that actualities were the proper materials for literature, he pushed further his inquiries into two sets of historical phenomena. That is, his studies in Diderot and the background of the French Revolution were accompanied by a growth of interest in the Scottish Reformation.[28] And he stated thus the reason for his interest in the Scottish Reformation:

> The History of the Scotch Presbyterian Church is noteworthy for this reason, that above all Protestant Churches it for some time was a real Church; had brought home in authentic symbols, to the bosoms of the lowest, that summary and concentration of whatever is highest in the Ideas of Man; the Idea unutterable in words; and opened thereby (in scientific strictness, it may be said) a free communication between Earth and the Heaven whence Earth had its being.[29]

A history of religious reform in sixteenth century Scotland, with its dramatic scenes, would have afforded excellent materials for Carlyle's three-fold fusion of history, religion, and poetry. And, in spite of his lack of the financial independence prerequisite for such a task, he felt an urge to make that subject into a book.[30]

In studying the Scottish Reformation, he was dealing with the history of the faith of his ancestors. And an element that he had in common with them responded to this study. Indeed, he and his mother had been reading together on the Reformation.[31] And the letter that he wrote on December 2 to his brother John in Rome must have seemed to John Carlyle like the voice of his mother speaking in modified language on a text centuries old in Scotland. For, after reporting to his brother on the deaths in the

---

[27] *Ibid.*, III, 178.
[28] *Letters of Thomas Carlyle to John Stuart Mill, John Sterling and Robert Browning*, edited by Alexander Carlyle (London, 1923), pp. 26 and 22.
[29] *Ibid.*, p. 26.   [30] *Ibid.*, p. 27.
[31] Froude, *Thomas Carlyle . . . 1795-1835*, II, 257.

neighborhood, Carlyle wrote a passage that shows the heart of the Calvinistic or Puritan view of life.[32]

What is this whole earth but a kind of Golgotha, a scene of Death-Life, where inexorable *Time* is producing all and devouring all? Happily there is a Heaven round it; otherwise for me it were not inhabitable.[33]

He resumed the topic later:

An eternity is already around us. Time (wherein is the disease we call Life), will soon be done, and then! Let us have an eye on that city that *hath* foundations.[34]

That is a special application of his notion of natural supernaturalism, which he had stated many times and which he stated again in the same letter.

I get more earnest, graver, not unhappier, every day. The whole Creation seems more and more Divine to me, the Natural more and more Supernatural.[35]

To him the Old Testament of the Hebrews was showing its deep meanings, as it had done to the Puritans.

Out of Goethe, who is my near neighbor, so to speak, there is no writing that *speaks* to me (*mir anspricht*) like the Hebrew Scriptures, though they lie far remote. Earnestness of soul was never shown as there. *Ernst ist das Leben*; and even to the last, soul resembles soul.[36]

His emphasis on the spiritual basis of life can hardly be repeated too often. Years before, at the beginning of his transcendental period, he had become permanently convinced of its fundamental importance. In the fall of 1832 he was well past the stage of abstract speculation on that principle. He was only examining the manifestations of the spiritual foundation in which he devoutly believed. And with that examination of the Scottish Reformation, which his earliest training had prepared him to understand, his Puritanic bias was growing.

At first glance it seems strange that Carlyle should see one leading truth under two such widely different aspects of life as the Scottish Reformation and the French Revolution. But to him,

---

[32] "Puritan theology was simply Calvinism, ultimately worn thin." *Encyclopaedia of Religion and Ethics*, edited by James Hastings (New York, 1919), X, 513, article on "Puritanism."

[33] Froude, *Thomas Carlyle . . . 1795-1835*, II, 257.

[34] *Ibid.*, II, 259.   [35] *Ibid.*, II, 258.   [36] *Ibid.*, II, 258.

both sets of phenomena were revelations of the supernatural in the natural. " *Ernst ist das Leben*; and even to the last, soul resembles soul." It is only the temporal parts that change. The French Revolution seemed to him

a stripping bare of the human soul: a fearful bursting out of the Infinite thro' the thin rinds of Habit. How do men act in these surprising circumstances? This is a question well worth asking. Should like to study it farther, far farther; and will try some day.[37]

He saw in the Scottish Reformation and in the French Revolution different aspects of the same thing. Both were revelations of the infinite in the finite. The Scottish Reformation was the constructive aspect: it had presented the infinite in authentic symbols, bringing the Infinite home to the bosom of the commonest man. On the other hand, the French Revolution was the destructive aspect: the traditional representations of the Infinite during the Ancient Régime had proved too restrictive, and " a fearful bursting out of the Infinite " had taken place. As Carlyle understood the trend of social developments in his time, both of these aspects were of great significance. He had previously concluded that the old frame of the society of his time was inadequate; and that it would have to be remade.[38] In the figurative language of *Sartor Resartus,* the death-birth of the Phoenix had to take place. The French Revolution seemed a historical example of the dissolution of old inadequate institutions. And the Scottish Reformation seemed a historical example of the palingenesis of adequate institutions. The obvious difference that separated a political and social movement from a religious and moral movement did not strike him as strongly as did the debatable element of their spiritual similarity. The reason was that he was pushing forward his fusion of history, poetry, and religion. He was preparing to give to history a dramatic presentation and a religious interpretation. Early in the new year 1833, he reported the progress of his studies in a letter to Mill:

[37] D. A. Wilson, *Carlyle to " The French Revolution," 1826-1837* (London, 1924), p. 311. This entry occurred on December 28, 1832. A similar passage on rending off habit occurred two weeks later, January 12, 1833, in one of his letters to Mill. (*Letters to Mill, Sterling, and Browning,* p. 33.)

[38] See, for instance, *Two Note Books,* pp. 183-184, and *Sartor Resartus,* pp. 196, 210, 212, 214-216

My Scotch Church-History studies have advanced a little; strangely blended with these French Anti-church ones; with which however they are not so incongruous as might seem.[39]

He considered Knox " a true Reformer, one of the sort much wanted now and always, seldom rarer than now." [40] So, strange as it may seem, Carlyle was seeing similar uses for both the French Revolution and the Scottish Reformation: they were both great lessons for the present.

Although his studies in two sets of historical phenomena had gone forward rapidly, as yet he had written nothing. His head was buzzing with the seen and the dim forecast of the unseen.[41] And he was troubled by more than one kind of confusion. In his notebook, he commented on his own state of mind:

To *teach* any of the things I am interested in were for the present impossible; all is unfixed, nothing has yet grown; at best, is but growing.[42]

Each one of the elements that were eventually to enter into the fusion of history, poetry, and religion was causing him confusion. And those troubles were further complicated by other considerations. His personal economic condition, as well as England's economic condition, was baffling. His own literary status, as well as the status of literature in England, seemed unpromising. But apparently the most stubborn of all those difficulties was the old problem of morals. Neither he nor the society of his time had been able to work out what he considered the proper moral system for the new era. Under those circumstances, the chief resource that he could call upon was his faith in a providential world-order. It was the faith of his fathers.

. . . I am very considerably bewildered; few landmarks in the Earth, yet God be thanked, some stars still shining in the Heavens: I can only say with the old Hebrew, in my own dialect, " *Still* trust in God, for Him to praise good cause I yet shall have ": so stood it in my Father's Psalm-book; pity for me if so much stand not also in mine! On the whole, in this wondrous condition of all things, Literary, Moral, Economical, there is need of courage, of insight; which may the bounteous Heaven, withholding what else it will, supply according to our need.[43]

---

[39] *Letters to Mill, Sterling, and Browning*, p. 34.
[40] *Ibid.*, p. 34.   [41] *Ibid.*, pp. 34-35.
[42] Froude, *Thomas Carlyle . . . 1795-1835*, II, 262.
[43] *Letters to Mill, Sterling, and Browning*, pp. 38-39: February 22, 1833.

Thus his own basic Puritanism or Hebraism deepened, even as he looked about him and in him for a new expression of its basic significance—a moral world order.

Fundamentally Carlyle was a moral reformer.

> That the Supernatural differs not from the Natural is a great Truth, which the last century (especially in France) has been engaged in demonstrating. The Philosophers went far wrong, however, in this, that instead of raising the natural to the supernatural, they strove to sink the supernatural to the natural. The gist of my whole way of thought is to do not the latter but the *former*. I feel it to be the epitome of much good for this and following generations in my hands and in those of innumerable stronger ones.[44]

But he was not attempting a philosophic presentation of the synthesis just mentioned. Instead, he was attempting to broaden and popularize that synthesis by a dramatic presentation and a religious interpretation of the actual life of man.

In the historical sketch of Cagliostro, which was finished by March 21, 1833, Carlyle seems to have had in mind that fusion of history, poetry, and religion. The important conclusions of Sauerteig, whom Carlyle again used as his mouthpiece, may be summarized as follows. The life of the meanest man is a poem. Only in reality lies the essence of all that was ever fabled, visioned, or sung by man. All history, all poesy, is but a part deciphered out of the rhapsodia of existence and rendered into the speech of man.[45] The manner in which men decipher this rhapsodia of existence is proportionate to their state of culture.[46] So far in the development of civilization there have been three original stages and consequently three different manners of reading the rhapsodia. The first stage was that of the earnest Orientals, the Hebrews, who read it wholly like a sacred book. The second stage was that of the other Orientals, of the Magi, of Zerdusht. Their gorgeous semi-sensual version, all defaced by time, has turned mostly to lies. One result is the Arabian tales. The third stage was that of the earnest West, the Greeks. Their version of the rhapsodia was the consecration of the flesh, which stepped forth life-lusty, radiant, earnest-smiling, in immortal grace, from under the chisel and the stylus, and intelligibly proclaimed the infinite.[47] Sauerteig then suggested a fourth stage, looking to his own times for a develop-

---

[44] Froude, *Thomas Carlyle . . . 1795-1835*, II, 267: February 1, 1833.
[45] *Essays*, III, 249-251.   [46] *Ibid.*, III, 252.   [47] *Ibid.*, III, 252.

ment beyond the three ancient manners of reading the rhapsodia of existence.

Of which three antique manners of reading, our modern manner . . . has been little more than imitation: for always, indeed, the West has been rifer of doers than of speakers. The Hebrew manner has had its echo in our Pulpits and choral aisles; the Ethnic Greek and Arabian in numberless mountains of Fiction, rhymed, rhymeless, published by subscription, by puffery, in periodicals, or by money of your own . . . . Till now at last, by dint of iteration and reiteration through some ten centuries, all these manners have grown obsolete, wearisome, meaningless; listened to only as the monotonous moaning wind, while there is nothing else to listen to:—and so now, well-nigh in total oblivion of the Infinitude of Life . . ., we wait, in hope and patience, for some *fourth* manner of anew convincingly announcing it.[48]

Presumably, Carlyle's fusion of history, poetry, religion was an approach to a fourth manner of reading the rhapsodia of existence. But while the fourth manner was being developed, there was great risk that the doctrine of natural supernaturalism would be misused and would degenerate into Eleusinian mystery or the unintelligible gift of tongues. Perhaps consciousness of that risk led him to add his distinction between the genuine man and the quack:

The Genuine, be he artist or artisan, works in the finitude of the Known; the Quack in the infinitude of the Unknown.[49]

Further, Carlyle assured the reader that his story of Cagliostro was the delineation of a reality, not a fiction, and that nature actually produced such a man.[50] And as if in answer to a question concerning the moral lesson of the piece, he added:

Foolish reader, in every Reality, nay, in every genuine Shadow of a Reality (what we call a Poem), there lie a hundred such, or a million such, according as thou hast the *eye* to read them![51]

Though *Cagliostro* was a first experiment in the practical fusion of poetry, history, and religion, Carlyle never used the term in connection with that piece. Rather, as will be shown, it was his next piece of writing that he looked upon as extensive enough and well enough executed to be considered as the first experiment.

During the period that he was occupied with *Cagliostro*, and for a considerable period thereafter, Carlyle found little encourage-

---

ment in his self-appointed task of presenting in moralistic literature the natural supernaturalism of history. His existence as a
writer still depended upon the approval of editor and readers. But
even in Edinburgh he was taken for a lost man; none would believe in him; and his heart was frequently overcast.[52] These were
the troubles of a prophet. And he met them in the attitude of a
prophet. His notebook entry of March 31 was characteristic:

Wait thou on the bounties of thy unseen Taskmaster, on the hests of thy
inward *Daemon*. Sow the seed field of Time. What if thou see no fruit
of it? another will. Be not weak.

Neither fear thou that this thy great message of the Natural *being* the
Supernatural will wholly perish unuttered. One way or other it will and
shall be uttered—write it down on paper any way; speak it from thee—
so shall thy painful, destitute existence not have been in vain. Oh, in
vain? Hadst thou, even thou, a message from the Eternal, and thou
grudgest the travail of thy embassy? O thou of little faith! [53]

By April 18 he had come to look upon pain as almost a necessary
precursor of new light. And he hoped only that his increase of
wisdom would be in fair ratio to the disquietude of the saddest
winter that he had known in a long time.[54]

The records of spring and summer, 1833, show a phase of his
progress toward a literature of " stern old-Hebrew denunciation."
Stiff-necked society, he thought, would suffer, since it would heed
neither revelation nor prophecy. Already his paternalistic tendencies toward government control were deepening. Organized emi-
gration under government control seemed to him the only way to
prevent an implacable rebellion of hunger and ignorance against
wealth and idleness, within the next few years.[55] He saw in the
terrible experience of France a warning for England in its present
social distress. But the French Revolution seemed to him a thing
utterly unknown in England.[56] The stern truth should be set before the English people in its true light. And he urged his friend
John Stuart Mill to undertake the task.[57] The age needed a literature of prophecy.

[52] Froude, *Thomas Carlyle . . . 1795-1835*, II, 279.

[53] *Ibid.*, II, 279.

[54] *Letters to Mill, Sterling, and Browning*, p. 47.

[55] *Letters of Thomas Carlyle: 1826-1836*, edited by C. E. Norton (London,
1889), pp. 355-357: March 26, 1833. *Letters to Mill, Sterling, and Browning*, p. 50: April 18.

[56] *Letters to Mill, Sterling, and Browning*, p. 51.

[57] *Ibid.*, p. 51.

> Alas, in these days, all light sportfulness, and melodious Art, have fled away from us, far away; not in Poetry, but only if so might be in Prophecy, in stern old-Hebrew denunciation, can one speak of the accursed realities that now, and for generations, lie round us, weigh heavy on us! [58]

Cromwell and Bunyan could have understood this passage. Both its form and pressure are Puritan.

So difficult was it for Carlyle to earn a living and at the same time to define and combine the need of society, the function of literature, and the duty of the literary man, that he sometimes felt like renouncing his whole vocation and emigrating to the new world.[59] But not knowing what to do, or how to do, he decided to wait-out the crisis. He would

> wait in a kind of *rest.* "*Halte still und seh' Dich um*": That is every way my posture at present. Outwardly and inwardly a kind of closing of the First Act goes on with me; the Second as yet quite *un*-opened. The world is fast changing, the ways and wants and duties of the world; I myself am also, or ought to be, changing: there must be a readjustment.[60]

Perhaps a short residence in Paris, the scene of the great exemplum of change, would have aided the readjustment of his ideas.[61] But that plan for change of outward conditions eventually came to nothing. On July 18, his correspondence with Mill touched again on the inner conditions of the crisis:

> spiritually too I told you I was at a kind of pause, a crisis; by God's blessing too I have no instant need to write aught in that humour; so I sit pretty quietly till the chaos lay itself, and the new *road* (for road there is for one in *every* case) grow plainer a little.[62]

The crisis, which had taken long to develop, did not pass easily.

Some passages written in the journal during the summer of 1833, about the same time as the passage just quoted, provide a more detailed index to Carlyle's mental condition. They show that, in the summer of 1833, he was putting himself through a severe cross-examination to discover the right road out of his perplexities.[63] What should be write? How should he present it?

---

[58] *Ibid.*, p. 48.   [59] *Ibid.*, pp. 53-54.

[60] *Letters of Thomas Carlyle*, p. 361.

[61] A plan for spending the summer of 1834 in France was mentioned in Mrs. Carlyle's letter of July 15, 1833. See Froude, *Thomas Carlyle . . . 1795-1835*, II, 285. See also *Letters to Mill, Sterling, and Browning*, p. 63.

[62] *Letters to Mill, Sterling, and Browning*, p. 63.

[63] Froude, *Thomas Carlyle . . . 1795-1835*, II, 281.

How should be interpret it? All of those questions arose in his mind. Although he had not yet decided on the French Revolution as his topic, he did aim vaguely at a large work—a book rather than an article:

Nobody asks me to work at articles, and as need does not drive me to do it for a while, I have no call in that direction. The thing I want to write is quite other than an article. Happily (this is probably my greatest happiness), the chief desire of my mind has again become to *write* a masterpiece, let it be acknowledged as such or not acknowledged. The idea of the universe struggles dark and painful in me, which I must deliver out of me or be wretched.[64]

Thus the specific subject of his would-be masterpiece still remained undetermined in his mind. Moreover, he was far from certain that he could command the literary method that he had hoped to develop.

I begin to suspect [he wrote] that I have no *poetic* talent whatever, but of this, too, am no wise absolutely *sure*. It still seems as if a whole magazine of faculty lay in me all undeveloped; held in thraldom by the meanest physical and economical causes.[65]

And the moral principle of tolerance, which he had thought should be interpreted to the new era by art and religion, was still giving him trouble. He discovered in himself too much of the intolerance against which he had for years struggled, and he believed that his own private discontent mingled with his zeal against evil-doers.[66] His confusion had reached down into his faith, which he felt had been in sad eclipse for a year.[67] But even that evil turned into a chastening rod and was good:

On the whole it is good, it is absolutely needful for one to be humbled and prostrated, and thrown among the pots from time to time. Life is a school: we are *perverse* scholars to the last and require the rod.[68]

Thus the stern Hebrew and Puritan Providence chasteneth whom He loveth. And even as Carlyle attempted to fight shy of Puritan intolerance of evil, his Puritan view of life became more fixed. Speculation always led him into contradictions.

Above me, as I thought last night in going to sleep, is the mute *Immensity*; Eternity is behind and before. What are all the cares of this

---

[64] *Ibid.*, II, 286: August 24, 1833.

[65] *Ibid.*, II, 282.

[66] *Ibid.*, II, 281-282.

[67] *Ibid.*, II, 286.

[68] *Ibid.*, II, 286.

short little Platform of existence that they should give thee Pain? But on the whole man is such a *Dualism*, and runs himself into contradiction, the *second* step he makes from the beaten road of the practical. I may lament meanwhile that (for want of symbols?) those grand verities (the reallest of the real) Infinitude, Eternity, should have so faded from the view, from the grasp, of the most earnest, and left the task of *right living* a problem harder than ever.[69]

It will be recalled that Carlyle's problem of morals was based upon that very Dualism. He had attempted to work out in his mind a new tolerant relationship between the dualistic elements good and evil, to replace the old hostile relationship between those elements. He had looked to German literature as a guide in the matter. But his own attempts had merely deepened his confusion. At each second step that his speculation took him beyond the beaten path of conventional morality, he had run into hopeless contradiction. With the lapse of time and the growth of his native Puritan bias, that new principle of morals seemed less promising.

On August 25, 1833, the day after the entry just quoted on life's confusing dualism, the American Emerson reached Craigenputtock. That transcendentalist-Unitarian would have been an apt listener to any exposition of the harmonious relationship of good and evil in a great organically unified whole. In fact he wished precisely such a exposition. Therefore he asked Carlyle to explain to him the religious developments toward which his essays " The State of German Literature " and " Characteristics " had pointed. Emerson himself reported the reply:

[Carlyle] replied that he was not competent to state it even to himself; he wanted rather to see.[70]

That reply has been too often considered modest. Instead it was merely candid. In August, 1833, Carlyle was becoming less and less able to understand the principle of morals that he had once valued in German literature highly enough to consider it the principle fit for the new era.

Though far from composure,[71] Carlyle's thought was growing

---

[69] *Ibid.*, II, 286-287.

[70] M. D. Conway, *Thomas Carlyle* (New York, 1881), pp. 220-221. Norton reads " waited " instead of " wanted " in the last clause of this passage. See: *Correspondence of Thomas Carlyle and Ralph Waldo Emerson 1834-1872*, edited by C. E. Norton (Boston, 1884, revised edition), I, 5.

[71] Froude, *Thomas Carlyle . . . 1795-1835*, II, 294.

more settled and more hopeful. On September 10, he wrote Mill about his condition, showing that some gain had been made.

For many years (seven, I think) the Pen has not been so long out of my hand as even now. A multitude of things required and require adjustment in me: it was a great kindness in my destiny too that precisely at this period I could pause without economical inconvenience; the first time I have had any inward wish to pause. I feel sometimes that I am not idle, tho' unemployed to the eye. We shall see what will come of it. In some week or two, however, I shall probably be again at my Desk; according to my old maxim that one should not puzzle, should not speculate; but having got even a little light, go instantly to *work* with it, that it may become *more*. I have a general feeling growing of late years that "I am all in the wrong"; and, by the Devil's malice, shall always have it, for we live in a Dualistic world.[72]

But as October began, he wrote his brother that he had not yet commenced writing, that the confusion within his mind was still too great:

The *new chapter* of my History as yet lies all-too confused; I look round on innumerable fluctuating masses; can begin to build no edifice from them. However, my mind is not *empty* . . . Alas, the *thing* I want to do is precisely the thing I cannot do. My mind would so fain deliver itself adequately of that "Divine Idea of the World"; . . . I want to write what Teufelsdröckh calls the story of the *Time-Hat*; to show forth to the men of these days that they also live in the Age of Miracle! We shall see. Meanwhile, one of the subjects that engages me most is the French Revolution, which indeed for us is still the subject of subjects.[73]

And in the same letter he indicated that his immediate task would be the writing of the history of the Diamond Necklace.[74] This affair was an episode on a stage set for the French Revolution.

As he approached the writing of history on the French Revolution, it is important to notice his statements concerning history,— particularly concerning the history of the French Revolution. These statements became more and more definite during 1833. In the essay "On History Again," published in May, he faced the problem that confronts all realists—the problem of selection and

---

[72] *Letters to Mill, Sterling, and Browning*, pp. 65-66. See also a letter to his mother on September 20 (Froude, *Thomas Carlyle . . . 1795-1835*, II, 297) for a hopeful note about commencing his writing soon.

[73] *Letters of Thomas Carlyle*, pp. 375-376.

[74] *Ibid.*, pp. 376-377.

compression.[75]   He met it with the doctrine of the survival of the greatest:

> ... men permanently speak only of what is extant and actively alive beside them.   Thus do the things that have produced fruit, nay whose fruit still grows, turn out to be the things chosen for record and writing of; which things alone were great, and worth recording.[76]

A principle of selection and compression, which Carlyle had always used in his writings and which he now enunciated with an appearance of logical reasoning, was the corrective that he needed for his theoretical tendencies toward pantheism in *Sartor Resartus*.   His notion of selection or compression shows too, but only incidentally, in his comment of June 13 on the revolutionary *mémoires* that Mill was sending him.

> A great result lies in these so intensely interesting Narratives; and *might*, had one the faculty, be drawn out of them; this were what I should call the highest kind of writing, far higher than any kind of Fiction even of the Shakespeare sort.   For my own share I declare I now enjoy no other Poem than the dim, shadowy as yet only *possible* Poem, that hovers for me in every seen Reality.   There is much here; of which I know not the limitations, the worth or unworth; meanwhile the feeling cleaves to me these many months, and seems decidedly to grow in me.[77]

In addition to the notion of selection, he there touched upon the old principle of poetic realism.[78]   The actualities of the French Revolution offered opportunities for the finest of poems, finer even than the fictions of Shakespeare.

A long passage in a letter to Mill on September 24 moved still closer to the fusion of poetry, history, and religion.   It showed Carlyle nearing the decision to write a history of the French Revolution.

> [The French Revolution] is properly the grand *work* of our era (a most sorrowful, barren and unfruitful work, yet still the work which was laid on us, which we have done and are doing): in this, in the right understanding of this, is involved all possible knowledge important for us; and

---

[75] I have not been able to discover when the essay " On History Again " was written.

[76] *Essays*, III, 174.

[77] *Letters to Mill, Sterling, and Browning*, p. 57.

[78] For the development of Carlyle's principle of poetic realism, see " Carlyle's Views of the Relation between Poetry and History up to Early 1832," *SP*, XXXIII (1936), 487-506 (above, pp. 37-56).

yet at the present hour our ignorance of it in England is probably as bad as total (for Error is infinitely worse than Ignorance); and in France itself knowledge seems only just beginning. *Understand* me all those sectionary tumults, convention-harangues, guillotine-holocausts, Brunswick discomfitures; exhaust me the meaning of it! You *cannot*; for it is a flaming *Reality*; the depths of Eternity look through the *chinks* of that so *convulsed* section of Time;—as through *all* sections of Time, only to dull eyes not so visibly. To me, it often seems, as if the right *History* (that impossible thing I mean by *History*) of the French Revolution were the grand Poem of our Time; as if the man who *could* write the *truth* of that, were worth all other writers and singers. If I were spared alive myself, and had means, why might not I too prepare the way for such a thing? I assure you the attempt often seems among my possibilities. The attempt *can* be made; cannot, by the highest talent and effort, be succeeded in, except in more or less feeble approximation. But indeed is not all our success approximate only? In any case I continue thoroughly interested in the subject, and greedily collect whatever knowledge I can get of it. That *Thiers*, these *Mémoires* of yours have done more for me than almost all else I had read; you can hardly conceive with what a tumult of feelings, visions, half-visions, guesses and darknesses they wholly envelop me.[79]

Although that passage stresses the poetic possibilities of the French Revolution as a manifestation of the supernatural in the natural, one element of the fusion is lacking. There is no allusion to the moral principle that had proved one of Carlyle's great problems for two years.

But the old problem of morality was very much evident in Carlyle's thought during the fall of 1833. His opinions on it were still divided. For example, the letter to Mill on September 24 showed a stern attitude on the issue. He told Mill that he set little store by the so-celebrated virtue of tolerance.[80] He felt that he had seldom seen real tolerance, but that he had often enough seen

Indifferentism parading itself in the stolen garments of it. "I came not into the world to bring peace, but a sword!" Such is in perhaps all cases part of the stern mission which a good man feels laid upon him. How different, above all, is that honey-mouthed, tear-stained, soup-kitchen

---

[79] *Letters to Mill, Sterling, and Browning*, pp. 70-71.

[80] *Letters to Mill, Sterling, and Browning*, p. 70. That reactionary viewpoint must have seemed oddly out of character in the Carlyle whom Mill had met and admired for his liberalism and tolerance two years before. In a letter to John Sterling in October, 1831, Mill had characterized Carlyle as having "by far the widest liberality and tolerance . . . that I have met with in anyone. . . ." John Stuart Mill, *The Letters of John Stuart Mill*, edited by Hugh S. R. Elliot (London, 1910), I, 16.

Jesus Christ of our poor shovel-hatted modern Christians from the stern-visaged Christ of the Gospels, proclaiming aloud in the market-place (with such a total contempt of the social respectabilities) : " *Woe* unto you, Scribes and Pharisees, *hypocrites* ! " Descend from your Gigs, ye wretched scoundrels, for the hour is come! [81]

A strong Puritanic bias is also noticeable in his comment to his brother John on art.

In my own heterodox heart there is yearly growing up the strangest crabbed one-sided persuasion, that all Art is but a reminiscence now, that for us in these days *Prophecy* (well understood) not Poetry is the thing wanted; how can we *sing* and *paint* when we do not yet *believe* and *see*? There is some considerable truth in this; how much I have not yet fixed. Now what under such point of view is all existing Art and study of Art? What was the great Goethe himself? The greatest of contemporary men; who however is not to have any follower, and should not have any.[82]

At last Carlyle had become conscious of a parting of his way from Goethe's way. Goethe was perhaps the chief guarantor, to Carlyle's mind, of the principle of tolerance as the moral principle of the new era. He was the man who, Carlyle had once thought, had left in his art works the rudiments of a ground-plan for the reconstruction of society. It had once seemed to Carlyle a noble task for men of letters in the next few generations to elaborate those rudimentary plans into a practical social framework. But a change had gradually come over Carlyle. Now he believed that Goethe was to have no continuator. Moreover, he thought it

[81] *Letters to Mill, Sterling, and Browning,* p. 70.

[82] *Letters of Thomas Carlyle,* p. 378: October 1, 1833. The same view was stated again in a letter to Eckermann on May 6, 1834. After admitting little concern with German literature during the preceding year, Carlyle nevertheless considered Goethe a great poet, who stood out more grandly as he himself increased:

> " yet stands out, as I might say, as an object *finished*, to which there will be no *continuation* made; like a granite Promontory, high and sheer, stretching far into the waste chaos; yet not thro' it; thro' it the world seems seeking itself *another* road, or losing all aim of any. To me most significant, forever *bedeutungsvoll, verehrungswürdig* ! "

He thought that, with Goethe, his labors in the German field might well end or at least pause. The fire was kindled: " . . . and thou take thy bellows elsewhither! This is one phase of the 'spiritual crisis' I spoke of . . ." (Thomas Carlyle, " New Letters of Carlyle to Eckermann," edited by William A. Speck. Reprinted from *The Yale Review,* July, 1926 [New Haven, 1926], pp. 9-10).

proper that he "should not have any." But in turning against Goethe the social prophet, he was by no means turning against Goethe the wise, sincere man.[83]

Whatever Carlyle said of Goethe, he was not willing or able to renounce entirely the principle of tolerance. That principle had become a part of his doctrine of great men,—heroes. Great men, however much at odds with conventional morality, must be justified. In the cases of all great reformers, moral force had broken the bounds of moral correctness.

Did *any* truly great man ever go through the world without *offense*; all rounded in, so that the current moral systems could find no fault in him? Most likely, never.[84]

Thereupon Carlyle stated again his great principle of tolerance for moral force. Just as when he had stated the principle in connection with Burns, he still believed that the index of morality lay not in the comparison of an individual's conduct and a fixed standard of propriety, but lay rather in the ratio between two variables,—his performance and his potentiality.

The thing is not only to avoid error, but to *attain* immense mases of truth. The ultra-sensual *surrounds* the sensual and gives it meaning, as eternity does time. Do I understand this? Yes, partly, I do.[85]

From the last quotation it is obvious that the principle of tolerance had become merged with the notion of natural supernaturalism. The complications were too great ever to be untangled. In short, Carlyle could not decide exclusively on either of the two moral principles, intolerance or tolerance.

On that problem of morals, as in most other matters, he eventually took up a practical decision rather than an entirely theoretical or rational one. He had speculated as far as was profitable to him. Already his speculation had done what, from the romantic point of view, it might have been expected to do. It had hindered his practice.

All barriers are thrown down before me; but then, also, all tracks and points of support. I look hesitatingly, almost bewilderedly, into a confused

---

[83] *Letters to Mill, Sterling, and Browning*, p. 79: October 28, 1833.
[84] Froude, *Thomas Carlyle . . . 1795-1835*, II, 300: October 28, 1833.
[85] *Ibid.*, II, 300.

sea. The necessity of caution suggests itself. Hope *diminished* burns not the less brightly, like a *star* of hope. *Que faire? Que devenir?* Cannot answer. It is not I only that must answer, but Necessity and I.[86]

The passage just quoted might be interpreted as referring to Carlyle's economic condition rather than to his mental condition if he had not been explicit in his letter to Mill on the same day.

I feel in general that I am at the end of an epoch, for good or for ill; if these disquietudes were but "growth-pains," how gladly should I bear them! All barriers seem *over-thrown* in my inward world; nothing is to *prevent*, to deter me, but also nothing to *direct*. I pause over a boundless, *unpeopled* prospect; ask how I am to walk and work there; *nehm' mich zusammen*. One of the questions that oftenest presents itself is, *How* Ideals do and *ought to* adjust themselves with the Actual? A vast question, as I take it up. On which ground our John Knox and Scottish Kirk is so peculiarly significant for me. A *genuine* Ideal, that did subsist, in spite of men and devils, with Life in it, for a hundred and fifty years! On the same ground too, my value for the Actual (in all senses), for what *has realized* itself continues and increases: and often I ask myself, is not all Poetry the essence of Reality (could one but get at such essence), and true History the only possible Epic? What limits my affirmative answer should have, are yet nowise clear.[87]

In that passage he indicated his procedure in the absence of the theoretical guidance that he had struggled for in vain. He could only hold fast to his belief in a spiritual world order, trust the principle that the greatest survives, and search in history for a clue to the ways of the future. Rather than to press further his conflicting principles of morality, he did the same thing that he had done when he wished relief from conflicting views in philosophy. That is, he took refuge in his old doctrine of Unconsciousness: the belief that true virtue, like true health, is not self-conscious. On November 1 he wrote this significant note in his journal:

Vain to seek a 'theory of virtue;' to plague oneself with speculations about such a thing.[88]

This was the cutting of the Gordian knot. He had not resolved the conflict. Apparently he never did resolve it rationally.[89] But by

[86] *Ibid.*, II, 300-301: October 28, 1833.
[87] *Letters to Mill, Sterling, and Browning*, pp. 79-80.
[88] Froude, *Thomas Carlyle . . . 1795-1835*, II, 301.
[89] Carlyle's apparent failure to reach a rational solution of the conflict between 1) the romantic principle of harmonious dualism and 2) the

thus dismissing it temporarily near the end of 1833, he gained freedom to write. Indeed, during the same month, November, he began his actual writing of *The History of the Diamond Necklace.*[90]

In *The Diamond Necklace,* finished by December 17, 1833,[91] Carlyle attempted to fuse history, poetry, and religion. The work was admittedly an experiment in French Revolution history, to see how far his method would carry. In *The Diamond Necklace* he pointed out the historian's duty of

---

Puritanic principle of hostile dualism may to some extent explain the fact that, in his later life, he simply retained two viewpoints concerning the relative value of beauty and goodness. For instance, in one of the lectures delivered in 1838, he presented Goethe as a writer who believed that "ideal art, painting, poetry, were . . . the highest things, goodness being only included in it." (*Lectures on the History of Literature,* edited by J. Reay Greene [second edition, London, 1892], p. 216). But at that time Carlyle spoke condescendingly of the belief. He mentioned it as only a curious opinion, which Goethe outgrew. (*Ibid.,* p. 216). On the other hand, apparently within a decade after that lecture, Carlyle talked to Espinasse " of the ultimate supremacy of the beautiful which, he [Carlyle] has also written somewhere [see *Essays,* III, 244], ' is higher than the good.' " (Francis Espinasse, *Literary Recollections and Sketches* [London, 1893], pp. 197-198). Furthermore, what Carlyle called the " litigation " between moral force and moral correctness was only another aspect of the same unresolved conflict. The litigation continued after 1835. For example, the doctrine of heroes, as it was enunciated in 1840, held up for admiration men who had the intellectual and moral force to discover new truth and to expand the old forms of propriety for the accommodation of it. Obviously the conception of the hero included the doctrine of tolerance. But during the same decade Carlyle's Puritanic cast of mind found expression in *Oliver Cromwell's Letters and Speeches.* Eventually Carlyle's " pure, *praiseworthy,* useful Hatred " showed its affinity with other similar Puritanisms. For example, in 1873, when he spoke of hell as a thing provided by the infinite love of God (see C. E. Norton, *The Letters of Charles Eliot Norton* [Boston, 1913], II, 19), the voice is the voice of Jacob and of Jonathan Edwards. However, even though the conflict was not rationally resolved, it is safe to say that, in many respects, Carlyle's Puritanism had been modified and wonderfully expanded under the influence of German thought. (See further, Professor C. F. Harrold's " The Nature of Carlyle's Calvinism," *SP,* XXXIII (1936), 475-486. Pp. 478-479 point out a change in Carlyle's Calvinism from 1840 on.)

[90] See Froude, *Thomas Carlyle . . . 1795-1835,* II, 301, and *Letters to Mill, Sterling, and Browning,* p. 87.

[91] *Letters to Mill, Sterling, and Browning,* p. 87.

looking fixedly at the *Thing*, and first of all, and beyond all, endeavoring to *see* it, and fashion a living Picture of it, not a wretched politico-metaphysical Abstraction of it. . . .[92]

Apparently the historian, the poet, and the revealer of the supernatural were to be considered the same:

What object soever he fixed upon, were it the meanest of the mean, let him but paint it in its actual truth, as it swims there [in time], in such environment; world-old, yet new and never-ending; an indestructible portion of the miraculous All,—his picture of it were a Poem.[93]

Carlyle continued, concerning the romance in reality:

. . . now, and formerly, and evermore it [romance] exists, strictly speaking, in Reality alone. The thing that *is*, what can be *so* wonderful; what, especially to us that *are*, can have such significance? Study Reality, he [the writer of this story] is ever and anon saying to himself; search out deeper and deeper *its* quite endless mystery: see it, know it; then . . . thou hast the firmest enduring basis: *that* hieroglyphic page is one thou canst read on forever, find new meaning in forever.[94]

And finally he added, concerning this particular story of *The Diamond Necklace*:

It is an actual Transaction that happened in this Earth of ours. Wherewith our whole business, as already urged, is to paint it truly.[95]

Although those passages indicate the fusion of the historical, the poetic, and the supernatural, they do not show the Puritanic bias that is to be found in many of his later writings. Apparently *The Diamond Necklace* was an experiment in depicting evil in others without illustrating malice or intolerance in himself.[96]

Carlyle's correspondence about *The Diamond Necklace* reveals a good deal of his thought. A letter written to Mill on the same day that this prelude to *The French Revolution* was finished shows, among other things, that Carlyle's speculations on morals had been accompanied by a deepening of his Puritanism. He commented thus on French character in general:

There never seems to have been in it [the French character] generally any *moral* basis, in our sense of the word (which I take to be a Puritanical,

---

[92] *Essays*, III, 326.
[93] *Ibid.*, III, 329.
[94] *Ibid.*, III, 329-330.
[95] *Ibid.*, III, 330.
[96] The same statement would hold good for his earlier choice of the quack Cagliostro as the subject of a sketch.

to be therefore an Old-Hebrew one, and of the greatest worth and depth),
but rather a quick graceful sensuousness. . . .[97]

The same letter defined history as a revelation of Providence:

[History] is an address (literally out of Heaven, for did not God order
it all) to our *whole* inner man; to every faculty of Head and Heart, from
the deepest to the slightest: there is no end to its purposes; none to
one's amazement, contemplation, over it.

And the first necessity in thus revealing the supernatural in the
natural was realism, as the letter further showed:

Now for *all* such purposes, high, low, ephemeral, eternal, the first indispensable condition of conditions, is that we *see* the things transacted,
and picture them out wholly as if they stood before our eyes; . . . You
must manage this by many indirect methods for yourself in your own
person.[98]

And in that letter, which announced the completion of *The History of the Diamond Necklace,* he described the piece as an attempt
at a poem.

I wanted to try whether by sticking actually to the Realities of the thing
with as much tenacity and punctuality as the merest Hallam, one could
not in a small way make a kind of Poem of it.[99]

A week later a letter to his brother John contained a similar comment on the historical piece.

My attempt was to make reality ideal; there is considerable significance
in that notion of mine, and I have not yet seen the limits of it, nor shall
till I have tried to go *as far* as it will carry me. The story of the *Diamond
Necklace* is all told in that paper with the strictest fidelity, yet in a kind
of *musical* way. It seems to me there is no epic possible that does not first
of all ground itself on belief.[100]

Finally, during the next summer, he dealt again with the same
subject in a letter to Emerson:

It is part of my creed that the only Poetry is History, could we but tell
it right. This truth (if it prove one) I have not yet got the limitations

---

[97] *Letters to Mill, Sterling, and Browning*, p. 83.

[98] *Ibid.*, pp. 82-83. See also in *The Diamond Necklace, Essays*, III, 326,
329, 330.

[99] *Letters to Mill, Sterling, and Browning*, p. 87.

[100] Froude, *Thomas Carlyle . . . 1795-1835*, II, 311-312: December 24,
1833.

of; and shall in no way except by *trying* it in practice. The story of the Necklace was the first attempt at an experiment.[101]

Thus, on August 12, 1834, Carlyle wrote of *The Diamond Necklace* as an experiment in unifying poetry and history. More than that, as has just been seen, it was an experiment in fusing not only poetry and history, but poetry and history and religion. For history " is an address (literally out of Heaven, for did not God order it all)."

Twenty days after the letter was written from London to Emerson, Carlyle began his writing of *The History of the French Revolution*. As he realized and pointed out, *The Diamond Necklace* was an experiment preparatory to the greater work. Although a detailed examination of *The History of the French Revolution* does not fall within the scope of this paper, that masterpiece of Carlyle's histories was also a fusion of religion, history and poetry. Except for an increased moralizing tendency, his method in it was similar to the method in *The Diamond Necklace*.[102] That is, both of them were dramatic presentations and religious interpretations of historical happenings. In both he was tracing out poetically, in actual human affairs, the ways of God to man.

This third article is an examination of Carlyle's practical working-out, by 1834, of principles that he had enunciated from a theoretical standpoint by early 1832. In the two preceding articles, we have seen those principles in some detail as they developed. It was

[101] *Correspondence of Thomas Carlyle and Ralph Waldo Emerson*, I, 24-25.

[102] Froude long ago called attention to the religious element in Carlyle's *French Revolution*: " he desired to tell the modern world that . . . God or justice was still in the middle of it, sternly inexorable as ever. . . ." (*Thomas Carlyle: A History of His Life in London, 1834-1881* [New York, 1884], I, 77). Professor Harrold has recently expressed a similar view concerning Carlyle's intellectual development between 1819 and 1834: " From first to last, he was the born Calvinist, seeking to reconstruct, largely from German thought, a belief in the transcendent sovereignty of Right and in a world of immanent divine law." (C. F. Harrold, *Carlyle and German Thought: 1819-1834* [New Haven, 1934], p. 235.) The last-named scholar may have had in mind the fusion of poetry and history when he wrote thus, concerning Carlyle's method in *The French Revolution*: " Aiming chiefly at pictorial effects he employed his style in an effort at dramatic vividness, and selected passages from sources according to its guidance." (" Carlyle's General Method in *The French Revolution*," *PMLA*, XLIII [December, 1928], 1167.)

partly because he had found the principle of tolerance more fully elaborated in Goethe and Schiller than elsewhere that Carlyle continued his interest in German literature long after his social and historical interests had begun their dominance. For a while he even considered the poet Goethe a social prophet. The poet was a man who dealt transcendentally with the actualities of human life and who gave them the highest moral interpretation. Thus, theoretically, poetry, history, and religion were fused. Poetry, Carlyle insisted, should find its materials in facts rather than in fiction. History the manifestation of the supernatural in the actual, was to serve as exempla to society. Religion, also a manifestation of the supernatural in the actual, was to provide the highest moral interpretation of these phenomena of life. But that problem of the highest moral interpretation caused him much trouble. It was one aspect of a conflict between two elements in his own nature—a conflict between romantic tolerance and Puritanic intolerance. At the death of Goethe in 1832, the tolerant viewpoint lost perhaps its ablest single supporter in Carlyle's mind. Even while he continued to regard Goethe as a prophet, Carlyle placed increasing reliance upon his own Calvinistic background. Thus the conflict became more baffling. Eventually, he ceased to believe that the social-prophet phase of Goethe was worthy of continuation. But both the romantic doctrine of harmonious dualism and the Puritanic doctrine of hostile dualism had become so deeply involved with Carlyle's other ideas, that he seemed unable to decide on either doctrine exclusively. Therefore he took refuge in the doctrine of Unconsciousness. Thus he interrupted what had become for him a very unprofitable speculation upon the abstract nature of virtue. At least he could fall back upon his doctrine of the historical survival of the greatest. Thus he began the writing of *The Diamond Necklace*. That work was an experiment in fusing history, poetry, and religion. It was the prelude to *The French Revolution*.